Trout

anglers, were well attuned to local differences between populations. 'After a time he knows that sound logic underlies their apparent caprice, and that the trout of different rivers are as various in their diet, their habits, their character and their appearance as are the races of mankind', wrote Holmes.[5] No longer restrained by the notion that animal species were divinely preordained, they came up with some interesting suggestions, none more ludicrous than the 'croaking trout of the Carraclwddy Pools' in Wales.[6]

Despite these shenanigans, a good number of the new descriptions survived. The 1941 edition of *The Observer's Book of Freshwater Fishes of the British Isles* lists ten native trout, among them the Loch Leven trout, the Orkney sea trout, the Sewen trout and the Welsh black-finned trout. Yet the number of 'varieties of this delightful fish' was far from settled, noted the author, A. Laurence Wells. 'Here we tread on dangerous ground. There is one school of thought that is of the opinion that there is just one species, *Salmo trutta*; there is another school that believes there are three species and yet another that holds to the view that there are ten.'[7]

Albert Flamen,
Trutta. La Truitte,
17th century,
engraving.

12

Gillaroo, one of the four types of brown trout found in Lough Melvin, Ireland.

Sonaghan, another type of brown trout found in Lough Melvin.

Fossils, the hard evidence for Darwin's theory, do not preserve well in fish compared to big bony animals such as dinosaurs. Of the trout's fossil ancestors that have been found, *Eosalmo driftwoodensis* is the most primitive that is known. Dating back 50 million years, its remains were first discovered in the 1930s in Driftwood Canyon, British Columbia. Less than 30 cm (12 in) in length, the Canadian lake-dweller apparently led the life of

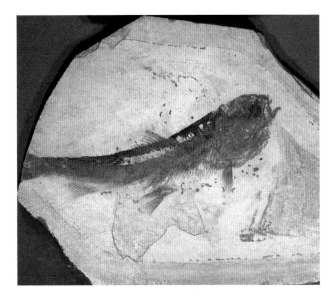

The earliest known fossil salmonid (*Eosalmo driftwood-ensis*), Driftwood Canyon, British Columbia.

a trout, not a salmon. Ranging in size from small juveniles to fully grown adults, the fossils indicate the fish spent all its time in freshwater. Ocean-going behaviour in salmonids evolved later – a development that spawned the prehistoric monster of the family, the sabre-tooth salmon (*Oncorhynchus rastrosus*). This twelve-million-year-old relative of the rainbow trout grew as long as an alligator and reputedly weighed up to 180 kg (395 lb).[12] However, despite an impressive pair of fangs, experts say it probably fed on plankton.

The modern-day trout is naturally distributed across the northern hemisphere and falls into two main groups: *Salmo*, the same genus as the Atlantic salmon; and *Oncorhynchus*, to which trout and salmon of Pacific origin belong.[13] The brown trout and related species are native to Europe, west Asia and northern Africa, from Iceland and the Atlas mountains in the

16

west to Siberia and Afghanistan in the east. The rainbow trout (*Oncorhynchus mykiss*), named for the iridescent magenta bands down its flanks, hails from watersheds of the Pacific rim, from the Kamchatka peninsula in northeast Russia to California. The rainbow's close relative, the cutthroat trout (*Oncorhynchus clarkii*), which ranges from Alaska south to New Mexico, has its major strongholds in North America's Rocky Mountains.

The *clarkii* of the cutthroat's scientific title remembers the historic Lewis and Clark Expedition of 1804–6 that first introduced white Americans to this 'Wild West' species. Actually it was Meriwether Lewis, not Captain William Clark, who, after a successful day's fishing, described in his journal an unusual trout with two red slashes under its jaw (hence the moniker).[14] This was by no means the earliest written record of this New World trout. Spanish conquistadors encountered the cutthroat in New Mexico in 1541, during Francisco Vásquez de Coronado's two-year search for the fabled 'Seven Cities of Gold'. Pedro de Castañeda, chronicler of that disappointed expedition, tells of a stream in the Pecos valley 'which abounds in excellent trout'.[15]

Rainbow trout (*Oncorhynchus mykiss*).

Today the Rio Grande cutthroat, a threatened subspecies, is honoured as New Mexico's state fish. The taxonomic confusion over the cutthroat mirrors that of the brown trout. Since splitting from the rainbow some two million years ago, its scattered and isolated populations have been a recipe for bewildering variety. The precise number of strains continues to be debated; however, Patrick Trotter lists twelve surviving subspecies.[16]

The rainbow trout is reckoned to encompass forms that include the redband trout and the California golden trout. The latter is a fish of such colour-saturated pizzazz that it would not look out of place on a tropical coral reef, though it in fact belongs in the alpine waters of California's Sierra Nevada range. Its Latin American counterpart, the Mexican golden trout (*O. chrysogaster*), is recognized as its own species.

The masu or cherry trout (*Oncorhynchus masou*) dwells at the other side of the Pacific, in Japan, Korea and Russia's Far East. The cherry trout (or cherry salmon – from the Japanese *sakura-*

Cutthroat trout
(*Oncorhynchus
clarkii*).

masu) is the sea-going version of the species, and is so named because it returns in spring when the cherry blossoms are out.[17] The resident freshwater fish keeps its youthful looks by retaining the dappling of 'parr' marks carried by juvenile salmon and trout into adulthood.

As for *Salmo*, the brown trout's genus, its speckled tribes are too numerous to list here. Taking a snapshot from southern Europe, there is the marble trout (*S. marmoratus*), endemic to Slovenia and Italy, which has joined up the trout's pattern of dots to create a uniquely marbled appearance. The odd soft-mouth trout (*S. obtusirostris*) of the western Balkans looks like a trout crossed with a grayling, sporting the latter fish's fleshy lips, underslung mouth and large scales. The Fibreno trout (*S. fibreni*), found only in Lake Posta Fibreno, Italy, is a part-time troglodyte that vanishes inside cave systems during dry periods. Scientists have yet to get to the bottom of these fish: a

California golden trout, a rainbow trout subspecies native to the Sierra Nevada mountain range in the USA.

new species of endemic 'dwarf trout' from Morocco's Atlas mountains was identified as recently as 2005.[18]

There are also salmonids, which, while not strictly trout, are commonly viewed as such because of shared physical traits and habitat types. The taimen (*Hucho taimen*), for example, is described as the 'world's largest trout' by the National Geographic Society, which has advertised it (for a 2009 television documentary) as the 'Mongolian Terror Trout'.[19] Better known to Mongolians as the 'river wolf', it can grow to weigh 70 kg (154 lb). A voracious predator with cannibalistic tendencies, the taimen's diet stretches to ducks, muskrats and ground squirrels.[20] The trout-like lenok (salmonid genus *Brachymystax*) of northern Asia is also called the Manchurian or Siberian trout.

A good proportion of these trout misnomers are North American. The brook trout and lake trout, really types of char (salmonid genus *Salvelinus*), were named by early European settlers after the Old World trout they had left behind. The pretty brook trout (*S. fontinalis*) that abounded in eastern streams and lakes made a fine substitute. The bull trout (*S. confluentus*) of the western us and Canada is a char too.

'Trout' was also applied to biologically much less appropriate American fishes: for instance, the largemouth bass (variously dubbed the green trout, bigmouth trout, pond trout and lake trout) and the saltwater weakfish (speckled trout or spotted seatrout). Other English-speaking colonizers named fish 'trout' that were not, wishful inventions that include the Indian trout (*Barilius bola*), a carp of fast-flowing streams in northern India, the zebra trout (*Aplochiton zebra*), found in the Falkland Islands, the spotted mountain trout (*Galaxias truttaceus*) in Australia, and a New Zealand 'sea trout' (*Arripis trutta*).

There are genuine sea trout in each of the three major trout groups that emulate the salmon's anadromous lifecycle. The sea

trout (brown trout), steelhead (rainbow trout) and coastal cut-throat (cutthroat trout) all feed at sea before returning to their natal rivers to breed. Sea-run trout were once thought to be distinct species. In *The Compleat Angler*, Izaak Walton refers to the 'Fordidge Trout', which is 'near the bigness of a salmon' and 'live their time of being in the fresh water, by meat formerly gotten in the sea'.[21] And he records 'Salmon-Trouts' in 'many rivers that relate to the Sea'.[22] Walton alludes to their migratory vigour in writing of trout that 'get almost miraculously through wears, and flood-gates against the stream; even through such high and swift places as is almost incredible'. Fishmongers continue to label sea trout as 'salmon trout', while regional British names include sewin, finnock, peal, herling and whitling. There is also a slob trout – a fish whose name suggests that it doesn't venture beyond estaurine waters because it can't be bothered. Yet to scientists they are essentially one and the same: anadromous brown trout (*S. trutta*). 'There are no real grounds for considering "sea trout" as anything more than brown trout in which the migratory habit is very well developed', W. E. Frost and M. E. Brown state in *The Trout* (1970).[23]

The brook trout (*Salvelinus fontinalis*) is really a type of char.

Bull trout
(*Salvelinus confluentus*).

The Aquaria Vattenmuseum in Stockholm, Sweden, has exploited the sea trout's homing instinct to create a unique visitor attraction. Each autumn, sea trout from the Baltic Sea leap up an artificial stream into an exhibition room full of aquaria fish. Here their wild migration ends, in a glass-fronted pool beneath a man-made waterfall. Sea trout, like salmon, spawn in the waters in which they were raised, but in the case of the Vattenmuseum trout the raising is done by staff who 'strip' the milt (sperm) and eggs of the returning adults by gently squeezing their sides. The resulting offspring are put on display before being grown on in large tanks. After two years, when the fish are at the 'smolt' stage and ready to migrate to sea, they are introduced below the indoor waterfall, where they are kept for a few days 'to let them know where they come from', as curator Robban Tranefalk puts it.[24] It is now that the trout imprint the scent of their tiny stream – a scent that Tranefalk says ought to be distinctive given all the plastic scenery and fake rocks. Even so, the fish must detect and recognize it from the faintest molecular signals during their journey back from the Baltic – a homecoming that could be as much as five years away.

In the wild, trout spawn in swift, shallow waters with well-oxygenated, clean gravels. Ripe females swell with eggs and shade darker in colour; cock fish add to their mating livery of bronze and copper tones a prominent hook, or kype, which protrudes from the lower jaw. This comes into play when they grapple over spawning territory. The female excavates a nest, or 'redd', for her eggs by turning on her side and thrashing her tail. Once satisfied with her work, she beckons the attendant male (or males) by arching up her head and opening her mouth. The pair, both quivering agape, release in unison.

The trout's most intimate moments were splashed in the papers in 2001, after revelations that female trout fake their orgasms. Under the headline 'Fussy fish fake it', the *New Scientist* reported that 'female brown trout do it too, to dupe potential partners into premature ejaculation. The trick may help females

Sea trout smolts being released at the Aquaria Vattenmuseum, Stockholm.

avoid mating with undesirable males or attract more partners'.[25] A team led by Erik Petersson of Sweden's National Board of Fisheries said that of the 117 couplings they observed, 69 resulted in false orgasms. 'She just stops the process', Petersson told CBC Radio's *As It Happens*. 'But the male, he is so excited that he misinterprets the female's cues and goes the whole way. He's a little bit tricked there.'

The translucent hatchling, 'alevin' or 'sac fry', emerges from its egg carrying an orange yolk sac, which sustains it through the early weeks. Alevins develop fins (including the curious adipose fin, a seemingly redundant nub of fatty tissue behind the dorsal fin of salmonid fishes) and generally become more trout-like as the yolk supply is used up. Becoming fry, they venture into open water to intercept tiny morsels such as midge larva. Scales form, as do red and black spots, and the thumbprint parr marks down each flank that characterize the next stage in the fish's development. As parr, trout and salmon look almost identical – those of brown trout and Atlantic salmon are indistinguishable to the untrained eye. Typically, fewer than three trout out of 100 will

Newly hatched trout alevins.

see their first birthday, and by the second year the chances are that only a single survivor will remain.[26] Of the two-year-old sea trout smolts released annually by the Aquaria Vattenmuseum, only about one in ten evade threats – which include anglers, cormorants, pike and sea eagles – to return as adults. The largest to date weighed an impressive 11.2 kg (25¼ lb).

A fully grown trout can be any size from that of a fairground goldfish to the proverbial whopper; it depends to a great extent on diet and the fertility of its waters. 'As some pastures breed

The largest Stockholm 'museum trout' to date – a male of 11.2 kg (25½ lb).

larger sheep, so do some rivers, by reason of the ground over which they run, breed larger Trouts', Walton observed.[27] The rivers that breed the fastest-developing trout are spring-fed and run over limestone or chalk. Classic examples are the chalk-streams of southern England. The high calcium content of their clear, alkaline waters promotes an abundance of hard-bodied invertebrates eaten by trout, from snails and freshwater shrimps to the rich assortment of aquatic insects to which anglers match their flies. Studies have shown chalkstream populations growing at almost three times the rate of their English counterparts in moorland rivers.[28] The biggest trout are fish-eaters that live in seas or lakes. Sea trout bulk up on baitfish like herring and sand eels to attain sizes that can dwarf a salmon. Records of huge brown trout hauled from European lakes include a 31-kg (68-lb) fish from Lake Maggiore, Switzerland, in 1928.[29] An even bigger monster of 42 kg (92 lb) is rumoured from Germany's Chiemsee. But the heavyweight champion may be the Caspian trout (*S. trutta caspius*), a brown trout subspecies found in the Caspian sea. Specimens weighing up to a massive 51 kg (112 lb) have been reported.

Trout have a reputation among fly-fishers for being fussy about what they eat. Certainly, they can be exceedingly choosy at times, confining themselves to one very specific food item. A rising trout might, for instance, vacuum up every female of the mayfly *Ephemerella ignita* in the final, egg-laying phase of its brief existence, but wholly ignore others of the species, never mind similar kinds of insects floating by. This 'selective feeding', where trout target a very specific food in an almost mechanical way, is explained by biologists as an energy-efficient hunting strategy. Generally, however, trout have catholic tastes and are opportunistic, as Beatrix Potter's Jeremy Fisher discovered while sitting on his lily pad. 'A great big enormous trout came up –

ker-pflop-p-p-p! with a splash – and it seized Mr Jeremy with a snap.'[30] He escaped minus his galoshes thanks to an unpalatable mackintosh – a means of protection the average frog plainly lacks. An instance of trout not being at all fussy was recalled in a letter to the *Daily Telegraph* from a reader who fished the river Dove as a child during the Second World War. 'One day, having run out of bread, my pal and I resorted to baiting our Number 16 hooks with the torn-off corners of Derby Corporation bus tickets (three halfpence at the time). Several unfortunate trout found them irresistible.'[31] Charles Kingsley, himself a dedicated trout fisherman, also paints the trout as a fish of unrefined

dining habits. In his Victorian children's classic *The Water-Babies*,
trout 'rushed from among the stones, and began gobbling the
beetles and leeches in the most greedy and quarrelsome way,
and swimming about with great worms hanging from their
mouths, tugging and kicking to get away from each other'.[32]

Whether gobbling leeches or sipping mayflies, trout rely on
a highly developed sense of vision. Frost and Brown write that
'the most noticeable features of the brain are the large optic
nerves . . . and there is plenty of evidence that trout have good
eyesight and can distinguish colours'.[33] That said, trout have a
distorted view of the outside world. Because of the way light
rays are reflected, refracted or absorbed in water, only objects

directly overhead are seen clearly. 'The fish lives, as it were, in a room with a ceiling made of mirrors except for a round skylight in the middle.' This watery distortion works both ways, helping to screen the trout from anglers and predators. Here the eyes have an extra function: acting as light sensors, they enable the fish to enhance its scaly camouflage by increasing or restricting the amount of dark melanin pigment in the skin cells to blend in with the riverbed or the hue of the water. Blind trout, unable to perform this chameleonesque trick, remain permanently dark in colour, leaving themselves badly exposed. The skin has another important defence role: approaching predators are detected as vibrations in the water by receptors around the head and along a row of modified scales down each side of the body, known as the lateral lines.

Anglers suppose that some trout are cleverer than others, the brown trout being the most challenging, and the cutthroat and

Linley Sambourne, 'Great trout rushed out on Tom, thinking him to be good to eat', illustration from Charles Kingsley, *The Water-Babies* (1894).

brook trout the least difficult to fool. Studies of fishing effort required per trout indicate that the cutthroat is up to twelve times more catchable than the brown.[34] Rainbow trout rank somewhere in the middle. Behnke says there is nothing obvious in the anatomy of the brown trout brain to indicate higher intelligence or reasoning skills.[35] The answer, he speculates, may lie in the retina of its eye: because it is better adapted to functioning in dim light, it is able to lead a more shadowy existence. The species is known for its crepuscular feeding habits, and for shady daytime hideouts such as undercut banks or beneath fallen trees. And perhaps experience has taught the brown trout to be warier than its peers. While America's indigenous trout have had just a century or so of significant angling pressure to contend with, Europeans have fished for brown trout with rod and line since at least Roman times.

SCIENTIFIC TROUT

The trout's popularity as a sporting and table fish recommended it as an object of scientific investigation. In the twentieth century,

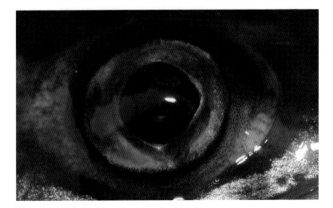

The eye of a brown trout.

30

its increasing commercial importance with the development of modern aquaculture, coupled with biologists' interest in comparative physiology (understanding and comparing how different organisms function), established the fish as a leading research animal. The rainbow trout, readily available from fish farms, became the white rat's aquatic counterpart. Scientists reported in 2002 that the species had been associated with no less than 20,000 studies in two decades.[36] 'It is without question that more is known about the physiology and phenotype of rainbow trout than any other fish species', they wrote. Used in a wide range of biomedical research, 'for many purposes trout may be a superior animal model than laboratory rats', concluded researchers working on the largest ever toxicology study involving animals.[37] In the 2009 study, scientists at Oregon State University exposed more than 40,000 trout to low doses of a cancer-causing compound to test a method of determining the level at which a carcinogen becomes a health risk. The advantage of trout over lab rats is that they can be used in large numbers at a fraction of the cost – in the case of this experiment, 'about 5 percent of what a rodent study would cost'. As well as its importance to cancer and toxicology studies, the rainbow trout is a human stand-in for research in immunology, nutrition and conditions such as heart disease.

The rainbow's ease of cultivation and the quest for bigger, quicker maturing stock led to the development of cloned lines, and has introduced the fish to the ethically murky waters of transgenic animals. Proposed 'super trout', laboratory-fattened using the DNA of other species, would yield extra meat and cost less in the supermarket. If some of the lumpy, muscle-bound prototypes look scary, more frightening is what might happen if they established themselves in the wild. However, in a strange twist, genetically altered trout may have a positive conservation role to play. They can be made to give birth to salmon, or vice versa, and in so doing, they may help to save the bluefin tuna. A team led by Goro Yoshizaki from the Tokyo University of Marine Science and Technology reported in the journal *Science* in 2007 that it had created masu salmon that produce rainbow trout offspring.[38] The salmon were engineered to become trout parents by implanting in them as hatchlings primordial sex cells taken from trout. These stem cells, which develop into either sperm or eggs, were accepted and incorporated into the salmon as if their own, but when they reproduced as adults, the result was healthy, 100 per cent rainbow trout. The goal is to apply the technique to breed threatened fishes from surrogate species. It is most likely to work for close relatives such as masu salmon and rainbow trout, species that diverged some eight million years ago. Similarly closely related species – the endangered Gila trout, for instance – have been identified as potential beneficiaries (and such fish could benefit even if they go extinct, because their

Trout stem cells being transplanted into a baby salmon.

stem cells can be frozen and kept in cold storage). Yoshizaki is attempting to replicate the salmon-into-trout trick with mackerel and their bigger cousins, bluefin tuna. This prized seafood fish has been decimated by overfishing, but so far scientists have failed to propagate it artificially. Since mackerel are small enough to keep in tanks, and a female can produce up to 500,000 eggs in one spawning, they could potentially generate hundreds of millions of baby tuna.[39]

ENERGIZING TROUT

Trout are putting their mark on another unfurling branch of science: biomimicry, or biomimetics, which borrows and takes inspiration from designs found in nature. In marvelling at the hydrodynamic perfection of trout, angler John Gierach observes, 'They are torpedo shaped, designed for moving water, and behave like eye witnesses say UFOs do, with sudden stops from high speeds, ninety-degree turns, such sudden accelerations that they seem to just vanish.'[40]

Inventors have been similarly struck by the fish. Those to have taken a leaf from it include Arno Boerner, a German who in 1927 launched the *Forelle* ('Trout'), a futuristic motorboat designed to mimic the fish's propulsion for greater speeds and fuel efficiency. America's *Popular Mechanics Magazine* reported, 'Boerner, of Dresden, has evolved a new type of boat that breathes water and even has scales along its sides. First tests showed that his boat developed extraordinary speed in proportion to its size and power.'[41] Said to use half as much fuel going at full throttle as standard models, the 9-m (30-ft) vessel drew water through an opening in its bow that fed two tubes containing turbine wheels; these then forced the water out from gill-like slits. 'His theory is that the fish take in water through the mouth, then compress the gill bags, to get pressure, and eject the water backwards through the gills, with the result that it covers the body with a thin sheath of water and eliminates the "skin friction" which holds boats back.' The thinking behind the 'scales' on the hull was that those of living trout create tiny swirls of water that help to propel them forward.

The trout boat prefigured the extraordinary contraptions of Viktor Schauberger (1885–1958), inventor, hydrologist, environmental visionary and pioneer of biomimicry. A forester by trade, Schauberger's observations of trout and their streams in the mountains of Upper Austria inspired his lifelong quest to harness Earth's natural energies for new technologies that were in harmony with nature. In the 1920s, while employed by Prince Adolph zu Schaumberg-Lippe as a forest warden, Schauberger identified a previously hidden counterforce in water that trout made visible. Later, when recalling the powerful influence of his forest experiences, Schauberger wrote of this mystical, midnight encounter:

It was spawning time. I took my post, on a clear moonlight night, close to a waterfall hoping to catch a fish poacher. I could see every move of the fish in the crystal-clear water. Suddenly, the fish moved toward the sides. A very large trout had come upstream. It swam along the fall as if in search of something, its motion like a winding dance, then finally disappeared beneath what looked like a sheet of glimmering metal under the moonlight. I noticed there was a whirlpool at the foot of the narrowing waterfall. The trout floated out of this vortex and up the waterfall as if drawn by an invisible force. Once at the crest, it was pushed out of the water and landed a few yards upstream. I was so excited by what I had seen I forgot all about the

Above, German "Fish Boat," Showing the "Gills" through Which It Sucks Water; at Top, Left, the Boat Being Launched in a Wheeled Cradle, and, Below, as It Appears When under Way

poacher and went home to think about it. I saw this pheno- menon many times after that, but no scientist could give me an explanation.[42]

Arno Boerner's 'trout boat', the *Forelle*, illustrated in *Popular Mechanics* (1927).

He likewise puzzled over how trout could lie for hours, almost motionless, in the fiercest torrents, and why, when frightened, they escaped by darting upstream, against the flow, not down. Schauberger's investigations linked the trout's current-defying ability to water temperature. He tested this by getting his men to heat up large vats of water which would be tipped in about

150 m (490 ft) upstream of an unsuspecting trout.[43] The concealed Schauberger watched as the fish struggled to maintain its position, its movements becoming ever more frenetic until finally swept away. 'Fish do not swim, they are swum', Schauberger concluded.[44] This was the trout's secret: it holds against the current by riding swirling vortices of cooler water, capturing their energy to slip like a bar of soap through wet hands. He further believed that to accelerate upstream they increase the 'squeeze' of the water by manipulating the flow through their mouth and gills to intensify the vortices travelling along their flanks. Schauberger sought to replicate the phenomenon in his 'trout turbine', or 'implosion machine'. It operated on his 'implosion' principle, whereby energy might be created by the cooling, inward-spiralling motion of liquids or gases – completely the opposite of the explosion-orientated, heat-inducing energy technologies we are familiar with. The device, which forced water through spiral-shaped pipes to create a self-sustaining vortex, was the power source for Schauberger's 'domestic power station'. 'The small output of an electric motor was multi-

'The Stationary Trout', from Callum Coats, *Living Energies: Viktor Schauberger's Brilliant Work with Natural Energy Explained* (1996).

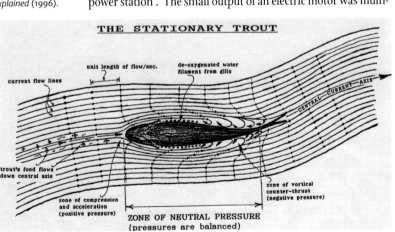

THE STATIONARY TROUT

unit length of flow/sec.

de-oxygenated water filament from gills

current flow lines

CENTRAL-CURRENT-AXIS

trout's food flows down central axis

zone of vortical counter-thrust (negative pressure)

zone of compression and acceleration (positive pressure)

ZONE OF NEUTRAL PRESSURE (pressures are balanced)

plied many times in a trout turbine, and used to drive a larger electric generator', writes Olof Alexandersson in *Living Water: Viktor Schauberger and the Secrets of Natural Energy* (1990).[45]

Schauberger's growing reputation led to an invitation to Berlin in 1934 from the Chancellor of Germany, Adolf Hitler.[46] 'What would be the source of fuel for your generators?' Hitler is said to have asked. 'Water and air; they contain all the power we need', Schauberger answered. Hitler promised the inventor 'all he needs to prove that he is right'; Hitler's sceptical scientific advisors, however, persuaded him to drop the offer. During the Second World War, Schauberger was pressed into service by ss Reichsführer Heinrich Himmler to develop new aircraft. Schauberger and his team – drawn from Nazi prisons – were based at Mauthausen Concentration Camp, near Linz. 'The project they initiated there was a "flying saucer" powered by a trout turbine.'[47] Surprising as trout-inspired Nazi flying saucers might seem, there is some evidence to suggest that the project got off the ground. Schauberger told the West German defence minister in 1956 that 'the first flying saucer rose unexpectedly, at the first attempt, to the ceiling, and then was wrecked'.[48] And in a letter to a friend he refers to a test flight near Prague in February, 1945, when a flying saucer 'attained a height of 15,000 metres in 3 minutes and a horizontal speed of 2,200 km/h'. Then there was his trout turbine-powered 'biotechnical submarine', designed to mimic the vortex-generating action of the trout's gills.[49] Also said to have caught the notice of the German military, Schauberger 'made it look as though it were not very useful, as in his opinion, bio-technology is for supporting progress and not for destruction'.[50]

These scarcely believable vehicles have disappeared into modern folklore. The story is they were destroyed, and their blueprints confiscated or stolen, at the end of the war. Schauberger's

legendary secretiveness and his intuitive, unorthodox working approach are other reasons given for the failure to replicate his machines. There are conspiracy theories, too: that the US Government and the powerful fossil fuel lobby deliberately suppressed his clean-energy inventions. Whatever the truth, Schauberger and his maxim, 'comprehend and copy nature', have a renewed following in this environmentally conscious age. Study groups investigate his principles and ideas, and once again his trout are inspiring technological innovation. Swedish company Watreco has come up with the Vortex Generator, a device which 'purifies water with the same forces a trout uses to stay steady in a rushing stream. Water gets poured in the top of the generator, swirls through an ever-tightening coil of channels, and then spits out the other end, fleeced of harmful chemicals and microbes.'[51] Researchers in the field of renewable energy are looking at

Viktor Schauberger with his trout turbine – driven domestic power station, 1955.

Viktor Schauberger, 'flying saucer' prototype, 1940s.

how trout exploit water vortices in order to develop urban wind turbines (these machines would capture the swirling gusts around large buildings), and for undersea generators that harness ocean eddies.

From models of Darwinian evolution and female deception in the battle of the sexes, to models for futuristic machines and green energy solutions, trout and their inner workings have exercised the human mind considerably.

2 Sacred Trout

Evidence of trout in human affairs goes back tens of thousands of years. Prehistoric fish bones in caves in northern Spain suggest that trout was already on the menu some 35,000 years ago. Sites that include the spectacular Tito Bustillo cave in Asturias, where more than 100 skeletal remains of *Salmo trutta* have been found, reveal the fish to have been a staple food of the earliest Europeans.[1]

The emergence of troglodyte trout-eaters may be significant: some scientists think that the consumption of fish helped our ancestors to gain an edge over Europe's native cavemen, the Neanderthals. Isotope analysis of fossil skeletons from the time when modern humans colonized Europe indicates that freshwater fish (revealed by high levels of the isotope nitrogen-15 in the bones) formed a considerable part of an increasingly varied diet.[2] By contrast, Neanderthals appeared stuck in their culinary and hunting ways; rather than take up fishing, they carried on chasing diminishing herds of reindeer, mammoths and other large herbivores – a strategy that possibly hastened their extinction. Maybe 'Neanderthals were unable to alter their subsistence strategies, whereas modern humans were more creative and were able to exploit resources more than the Neanderthals', say the anthropologists who undertook the dietary study, Michael Richards and Erik Trinkaus.[3]

The identification of trout in Palaeolithic art is not clear-cut. Fish carvings on portable objects like antler batons typically resemble salmonids, but it is hard to say which species they depict. In cave art, salmon and trout were overshadowed by the big prehistoric beasts: mammoths, bison, bears, woolly rhinos and so on. 'Salmon probably feature infrequently because they were so common', writes Peter Coates. 'Cave art usually depicted the most feared and highly prized of animals.'[4] However another Spanish cave, El Pindal, contains what may be the earliest known rock art trout. Dating to the last ice age, the engraving is described as looking like a cross between a trout and a tuna.[5] An ice age tuna with an adipose fin and red markings is perhaps the more fanciful explanation, especially since tuna are oceanic fish and would have been quite a distance from the sea (because sea levels were about 140 m/460 ft lower then).

HOLY TROUT

In ancient Europe, trout enjoyed cult status – a cult that persisted as a relic of mysterious, water-related belief systems long after Christianity's arrival. 'Traces of these beliefs remain in the form of sacred fishes in holy wells, which in some instances were present until recent times', write Janet and Colin Bord in *Sacred Water: Holy Wells and Water Lore in Britain and Ireland* (1985).[6] Hallowed trout abounded in holy wells and springs, usually in association with early saints and places of pilgrimage – Christian missionaries well understood the advantages of incorporating popular elements of native faiths into the new religion.[7] Take, for example, the miracle-performing trout of the Welsh hamlet of Nant Peris. Legend has it that the fish were installed there by Peris, an obscure sixth-century saint. Belief in their healing powers had people queuing up – 'rickety children and

scrofulous and rheumatic persons' – until the 1850s, according to *Lives of the British Saints* (1913).

A Celtic trout figure, which decorated a hanging bowl, late 6th to early 7th century, found at Sutton Hoo, England, in 1939.

The tradition is that if one of the fish came out of its hiding place when an invalid took some of the water for drinking or for bathing purposes, cure was certain; but if the fish remained in their den the water would do those who took it no good . . . Two fish only are to be put into the well at a time, and generally they live in it for about half a century. If one dies before the other, it would be of no use to put in a new fish, for the old one would not associate with it, and would die. The experiment has been

The painted engraving of a trout wearing a golden chain, Peterchurch, Herefordshire, England.

tried. The last of the two fish put in the well about fifty years previously died in August 1896. It had been blind for some time. It measured 17 inches.[8]

It is said that the Welsh adorned their sacred trout with gold rings. A fine illustration survives just across the English border in Peterchurch, where a stone engraving in the village church depicts a portly specimen in a gold chain, like some well-to-do alderman. According to local lore, the fish (its age is uncertain though it was painted and gilded in the 1820s) commemorates a trout that once lived in the Golden Well, source of the river Dore. Others say the trout was kept in nearby St Peter's Well – supposedly consecrated by Peter the Apostle while over on missionary work. 'Having blessed it, he used the water for baptising those he converted. One day a large fish appeared in the hallowed spring, which Peter secured with a golden chain.'[9] Pilgrims and cure-seekers would put money in a wooden box for an audience with the trout.

If well trout were a money-spinner for the church, their main practical purpose was to ensure the purity of the water, writes David Profumo. Besides keeping wells clear of insects, 'the trout was also an indication that the water was clean; thus their function was similar to that of a canary down a mine-shaft'.[10] Martin Martin, author of *A Description of the Western Islands of Scotland* (1703), records visiting such a trout on the Isle of Skye during his travels in the islands in the 1690s.[11] 'The Natives are very tender of it, and tho' they often chance to catch it in their wooden Pales, they are very careful to preserve it from being destroy'd, it has been there for many Years.' Martin noted a similar attitude towards the trout of Skye's Loch Siant. 'It abounds with Trouts, but neither the Natives nor Strangers will ever presume to destroy any of them, such is the esteem they have for the Water.' Trout apparently also had a role in Hebridean sorcery. An envious neighbour might steal the milk supply of someone's cow for their own less productive beast by secretly washing its owner's

Tobernalt Holy Well, 1930s.

45

milk pails 'in the Rivulets where Trouts are'.[12] Martin says the spell could be reversed 'by taking a live Trout, and pouring Milk into its mouth'.

Many Irish neighbourhoods had wishing well trout. Those of St Ciaran's Well, near Kells, 'could only be seen at midnight on the first Sunday in August, and the pilgrims used lights to try and catch a glimpse of them'.[13] W. G. Wood-Martin's *Traces of the Elder Faiths in Ireland* mentions two County Sligo wells: Tobernalt (or Tubbernalt), whose fish were reputed to restore sight to the blind, and Tubber Tullaghan, where 'there is a brace of trout, not visible to ordinary eyes, but which people living declare they have seen'.[14] In County Cork, it was a tradition on fasting days to throw the trout of a sacred lough basketfuls of bread and biscuits. 'Cures of every kind were effected by the potency of the waters, and as usual, the period of devotion was always closed by revelry.'[15] Wood-Martin says Irish 'fish worship' (salmon and eel were the other top fishes of devotion) continued until the nineteenth century, when it was still customary for pilgrims making the barefooted trek up Croagh Patrick mountain to pay homage to the trout of 'Aughawhale'.

> They pick up baits and throw them into the water, and it is the most lucky omen in the world to them if a trout come out and eat the bait, but if not, they cry out to St Columbkille to send [the fish] out. If they do not appear, there is some misfortune to come upon them, with loss of friends and relations.[16]

The author, writing in 1901, adds, 'Any person who will take the trouble to examine carefully a few holy wells will find pieces of bread in the water, thrown in as offerings to their sacred piscine inhabitants.'

The unusual stripes or dark markings that were sometimes observed on these trout gave rise to stories that went along similar lines: 'The progenitors of these fish had been caught, by unbelievers, and placed on a gridiron to fry. No sooner, however, had they touched the iron than they were mysteriously transported back again into the cooling waters of the sacred spring, but they still retain marks of the fire and of the gridiron.'[17] One such legend, the White Trout of Cong, concerns a subterranean fairy fish, totally white but for a red splash on its side. Caught by a godless soldier, who, on returning home, starts cutting it up for dinner, the trout transforms into 'a lovely lady – the beautifullest young crathur that eyes ever seen, dressed in white with a band o' goold in her hair, and a sthrame o' blood runnin' down her arm'.[18] The legend features in W. B. Yeats's anthology of Irish folklore, *Fairy and Folk Tales of the Irish Peasantry* (1888), and is echoed in his poem 'The Song of Wandering Aengus'. It begins:

> I went out to the hazel wood,
> Because a fire was in my head,
> And cut and peeled a hazel wand,
> And hooked a berry to a thread;
> And when white moths were on the wing,
> And moth-like stars were flickering out,
> I dropped the berry in a stream
> And caught a little silver trout.[19]

The trout symbolized health and fertility in ancient Europe, as represented in this Celtic-style design.

The trout becomes 'a glimmering girl with apple blossom in her hair', who, calling the poet's name, 'ran and faded through the brightening air'. Wrapped here in Irish mythology, Yeats's unrequited love and lifelong muse, the beautiful Irish revolutionary Maud Gonne, here becomes a shape-shifting goddess. Yeats, in his notes on the poem, refers to the descendents of the Celtic goddess Danu, the mother of gods, who 'in the waters take often the shape of fish'.[20]

Certain fertility rites also invoked the trout, writes Profumo:

The ancient Celts celebrated the rebirth of the sun and the passing of the dead months of winter with a dance of 'the springing trout', wherein the leaping fish-dancers imitated the rising fish to represent the sun rising from the water. The trout as a motif of health and fertility is a familiar one in European culture.[21]

There is plenty of evidence in the British Isles for the veneration of gods linked to water and the underworld.[22] Prehistoric monuments, including long barrows and megalithic circles, are commonly associated with rivers and springs. Silbury Hill, Europe's largest prehistoric mound, was built at the springhead of the river Kennet, while excavations at Stonehenge between 2004 and 2009 explained the monument as part of a much larger ritual complex centred around the headwaters of another chalk-fed river, the Avon.[23] That these two rivers are prized for their trout may not be coincidental. It does not take a great leap of the imagination to understand how the fish might have been seen as the embodiment or guardian spirits of pure, constant waters that rose magically from the earth. For people whose belief systems were rooted in the nature, perhaps trout were an important indicator species – something we have again begun to recognize today.

On the other side of the world, the aboriginal Ainu of northern Japan believed the planet owed its very foundation to a trout. It was their 'backbone fish of the world', revealed John Batchelor, a nineteenth-century English missionary who spent 60 years living among the Ainu on Hokkaido island, and who left an

important record of their culture and language before the Ainu were swallowed up by the ethnic Japanese.[24] Unlike the Japanese, who thought the earth was flat, the Ainu saw it as round, and resting on the back of an almighty trout. Batchelor translates an oral account of their creation myth (an interpretation that is perhaps coloured by his own Christian faith):

> Before God made the world there was nothing but swamp to be seen, in which, however, there dwelt a very large trout. This trout was indeed a mighty fish, for his body reached from one end of the swamp to the other. Now, when the Creator produced the earth He made the creature to become its foundation. There lies the living trout beneath the world, taking in and sending out the waters of the sea through his mouth. When he sucks the water in, the ebb of the tide takes place, but when he sends it out the tide flows.[25]

The great fish was responsible for major acts of God.

> The trout upon whose back the world is founded is the cause of tidal-waves. Every now and again he takes in vast quantities of water, and then with an extraordinary effort shoots it out of his mouth in one mighty blow of his breath. It is this which makes the tidal-waves. So, again, when he shakes himself the consequence is an earthquake. When he moves gently the earthquake is small, but when he is angry and moves furiously it is great.

To mitigate the threat, a pair of deities was assigned to the fish to hold it down and stop it wriggling about too much. Not surprisingly, the Ainu equivalent of the Loch Ness Monster also took

There are also sacred trout in Western Asia. At the ancient city of Urfa, Turkey, pilgrims still pay their respects to the trout and carp that dwell in a holy, spring-fed pool that is bordered by mosques.

the form of a trout. The lake creature would lie in ambush near
the water's edge; people, bears and even fishing boats were eaten
whole. Batchelor says the Ainu took the legend seriously enough
'to have a special dread of large lakes'. One of these giant trout
was said to have washed up on the shores of Lake Shikotsu (or
Chitose) in the seventeenth century: 'This monster had swallowed a large deer, horns and all; but the horns caused a severe
attack of indigestion to come on, which the fish could not get
over.'[26] The Ainu were both animalists, who believed all living
things possessed a divine spirit, and expert fishermen. Trout,
along with salmon, were a staple food and integral to their way
of life, which may explain why the fish featured prominently in
their religious mythology. Batchelor says that salmon and trout

'were reckoned as the chief of fish and were called gods in a sense often rather more honourable than that of mere courtesy'.[27]

Actually, a trout monster choking to death on a deer is not as far-fetched as it sounds. Hokkaido is home to the Sakhalin taimen (*Hucho perryi*), a voracious salmonid which reputedly can live to more than 40 years and grow to 90 kg (198 lb).[28] The closely related species *H. taimen* is thought to be behind persistent legends of water monsters in Lake Kanas in northwest China, and the same fish in Mongolia (introduced in chapter One as the 'Mongolian terror trout') is known for taking very large mouthfuls: a now illegal fishing method involves throwing out a giant hook baited with a ground squirrel.

Endangered by poaching and pollution, the Mongolian taimen in 2002 became the focus of a faith-based conservation project that has linked its fortunes with a Buddhist revival in the country.[29] The Tributary Fund, a Montana-based charity that engages the religious beliefs of indigenous cultures in the cause of conservation, teamed up with Buddhist leaders in a bid to save the taimen of northern Mongolia's Üür river. The programme included rebuilding the Dayan Derkh monastery, one of hundreds of Buddhist monasteries destroyed in the 1930s on the orders of Mongolia's communist dictatorship. Since the demise of the Soviet-backed regime in 1990, Buddhism, with its reverence for all living things, has re-emerged. The taimen is revered 'as the children of a strong river spirit', says one biologist on the team.[30] The project received an extra fillip, the *Wall Street Journal* reported, when local monks rediscovered a long-lost sutra, warning that 'for every fish killed, 999 human souls will suffer'.[31] The restored monastery, completed in 2006, is now able to spread the word. Funding comes from a novel partnership with fishing

The legendary taimen, which draws Western anglers to Mongolia.

tour operators that bring Western anglers in pursuit of the fish of their dreams. Concession fees go towards the cost of conservation work and anti-poacher patrols along the river. Saving the taimen by encouraging people to catch them might seem like a contradiction, but single, barbless hooks are used, and anglers keep only photos of their prize catch – the fish are carefully released. And if Buddhist strictures against doing unnecessary harm to nature pose a moral dilemma, the monks, seeing the greater cause, let it pass.

HAIRY TROUT

The 'hairy trout' – a species whose existence cryptozoologists do not rule out – originated in Iceland. Known as *lodsilungur*, the hirsute salmonid was attributed to Norse giants and demons who sent it 'as a punishment for some human wrongdoing. Sometimes lakes and rivers were full of fins and hairy trouts, which were considered totally useless and a kind of noncatch,' writes Icelandic anthropologist Gísli Pálsson.[32] Fins (a poisonous, backwards-swimming fish with reversed fins) and hairy trout were malevolent water-beings associated with poor or inedible catches. Aquatic beasts flourished in the mythology of this barren land of fire and ice, where terrestrial animals are thin on the ground. For a people who reaped waters, not fields, fish were a preoccupation; they 'for a very long time played a great part in the popular fancy, and many a strange idea concerning them has taken hold on the ordinary mind'.[33]

A natural explanation for this is offered by *Saprolegnia,* a white, woolly mould that feeds off the skin and flesh of salmon and trout in freshwater. Spawning fish, physically spent and their immune systems weakened, are most prone to infection. The fungus-like growth spreads over them in a ghostly cloak. Though alive, the fish are rotting away; the meat is no good for eating – a bad omen indeed for medieval subsistence fishers.

Hairy trout later developed a wider distribution, spreading to North America. Known there as the furry or fur-bearing trout, sightings of the animal have been reported in rivers and lakes in northern Canada, the Great Lakes area, and the Rocky Mountains. Sources include a tongue-in-cheek article in the *Pueblo Chieftain* in 1938 about fur-bearing trout near Salida, in Colorado's Arkansas river. A request for proof of the animal's existence – the result, some claimed, of a hair tonic spillage incident – had been received from a citizen of Pratt City, Kansas. In response, Salida's chamber of commerce 'dispatched posthaste a photograph of the fish . . . and told the Kansan to use his own judgment as to the authenticity of the species'.[34] It doubtless resembled one of the dubiously pelted exhibits once popular with American curiosity museums and circus sideshows; these were entirely suggestive of normal fish to which mammal fur had been glued. Their human counterpart would be the Abominable Snowman. The usual explanation given is that the trout evolved hair as insulation against the extreme cold of northern waters.

'Hicken's Fur Bearing Trout', which was allegedly caught in Iceberg Lake, Montana, 1920s.

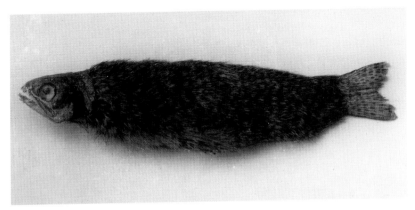

Nutrition Facts
Serving Size 1/4 cup (55g)
Serving Per Container: About 6

Amount Per Serving

Calories 79 Calories from Fat 34

	% Daily Value*
Total Fat 3g	5%
Saturated Fat 1g	6%
Cholesterol 82mg	20%
Sodium 202mg	9%
Total Carbohydrate 0g	0%
Dietary Fiber 0g	0%
Sugars 0g	
Protein 19g	

Vitamin A 0% • Vitamin C 0% • Calcium 15% • Iron 6%

*Percent Daily Values are based on a 2,000 calories diet. Your daily values may be higher or lower depending on your calorie needs.

CONEY ISLAND

® *Brand*

YAMADA

EXTRA FANCY CANADIAN

HAIRY TROUT

NET WEIGHT 19 OZ. (425 g)

Takeshi Yamada

70974 96013

'Coney Island Brand Exotic Canned Food #70', 2005.

   An early account of this shaggy trout story appeared in May 1929, in the Montana State Fish and Game Department's *Montana Wild Life*. Describing a successful fishing trip to Iceberg Lake, Glacier National Park, the author writes, 'They make a rare fight in landing them out of the water, due to the fact that nature has provided them with this fur, which ruffles and causes such a resistance that it is practically impossible to land them.'[35] New York artist Takeshi Yamada, whose 'rouge taxidermy' series recreates the unnatural wonders of freak shows past, has kept the tradition going with works including *Canadian Hairy Trout* (2004). The fish is also available tinned, part of Yamada's *Coney Island Brand Exotic Canned Animal* collection. The product label reads 'Extra Fancy Canadian Hairy Trout'. From sacred trout to canned freak trout – our cultural response to the animal has certainly changed over time.

3 Imperial Trout

Native to the northern hemisphere, today trout inhabit every continent bar Antarctica. Introduced to Argentina, Australia, Bhutan, Chile, India, Ethiopia, New Zealand, South Africa and wherever else suitable waters could be found, our passion for trout knows no bounds.

Where the white man went, so did his trout. A former great empire, vanished from the world map it once coloured red, can be traced by the fish it left behind. The British, in making themselves at home in far-flung territories, liked to install their favourite animals. Game such as partridge, hare, red deer and, if at all feasible, trout, were a comfort to them in foreign lands. Discovering large areas of unpopulated trout habitat (indigenous, non-trout fishes hardly counted), nineteenth-century colonialists completed what they saw as nature's unfinished work. Arguably the British Empire's major legacy animal, the sun never sets on the imperial trout.

The European brown trout was launched on the wider world in 1864, the year it was shipped 12,000 miles (19,300 km) from London to Australia. As Jean Walker relates in her history of the incredible endeavour, *Origins of the Tasmanian Trout* (1988), the original aim was to transport live Atlantic salmon to Tasmania. Authorities there wanted to establish a salmon fishery, and they even planned to import Britons to catch them: '35 married salmon fishermen – men of good character and industrious habits', a Tasmanian Government feasibility study recommended.[1] The first attempt was made in 1852 when a 454-ton barque, the *Columbus*, set off loaded with 50,000 salmon ova. The eggs were placed in gravel in a large, lead-cased tub that held 60 gallons (270 litres) of water. But the rise in temperature in the tropics caused the ova to hatch far too early; the tub turned tepid and cloudy, 'and when the water cleared again in colder latitudes, nothing could be seen'. The fish had vanished into the equatorial ether. The failure, says Walker, taught the would-be fish introducers two lessons: that the eggs 'must be shielded from concussion' (caused by the swell of the ocean); and that a low water temperature must be maintained throughout the voyage. 'These two conditions appeared to present an almost insurmountable obstacle.' The challenge fell to Sir James Youl, a retired Tasmanian farmer living in England, where he acted as an agent for the colony. Recruited to carry the project forward, he would later be recognized for his 'untiring zeal and indefatigable exertions' and for 'one of the most valuable discoveries ever yet made in the art of pisciculture'.[2]

Youl developed a system of egg trays that could swing with the motion of the vessel while being cooled by water from melting ice. The equipment was installed on the US clipper *Sarah Curling*, which embarked from Liverpool in February 1860. However the ice – all 15 tons of it – melted quicker than anticipated, and by the 59th day all the salmon ova were dead. Robert Ramsbottom, the pisciculturist who had supplied the salmon eggs, told Youl: 'You might as well try to fetch Australia to England as to carry spawn to it . . . Neither one man nor another can carry living ova to Australia in any way.' But Youl, who epitomized the Victorian can-do spirit, got to work on the next attempt, assisted by additional funding from

Victoria and from South Island, New Zealand, colonies which had salmon fishery ambitions of their own.

A larger icehouse with a holding capacity of 25 tons was built on the steamer *Beautiful Star*. Youl modified his tray system so that at least 500 gallons (2,300 litres) of cold water flowed over the eggs daily. As an experiment, he also packed a handful of ova in moss in a small box.[3] Departing from London in March 1862, the voyage was doomed from the start. Terrific storms in the English Channel resulted in a three-week delay, after which the steamer was forced to put back to the Scilly Isles for repairs. Again, the ice store melted and the cargo perished. The last of the ova to die, 74 days into the journey, were in the box of moss. This latest costly failure did not go down well. Arthur Nicols, in *The Acclimatisation of the Salmonidae at the Antipodes* (1882), says that Youl was 'was abused by the majority of the colonists and the colonial press, and accused of having wasted the public funds on a crochet'.[4]

The rather optimistically titled Salmon Commissioners of Tasmania convinced the island's government to allow Youl another shot. Relocating his experiments to the London vaults of the Wenham Lake Ice Company, which operated out of Massachusetts, he dropped his complicated swinging trays, tanks and pipes, and instead focused on refrigerated moss boxes. Youl found that if the moss died, so did the salmon eggs; however, by burying the boxes deep under the ice he succeeded in delaying hatching of the ova to 100 days – time enough to reach Tasmania. Space was donated for the shipment by the owners of the *Norfolk*, a three-masted wooden clipper. Built for the emigrant trade and, according to Walker, 'one of the fastest ships on the England-Australia run', she was the perfect conveyance for the embryonic fish migrants. They travelled in 181 pine boxes measuring 30 × 22 × 13 cm (11 × 8 × 5 in). Perforations allowed meltwater from the ice – piled to a height of 2.7 m (9 ft) on top of them – to trickle through. Resting on a bed of charcoal, the moss was laid carefully between two layers of crushed ice. Sealed with screwed lids, the boxes contained more than 100,000 salmon eggs.

Shortly before the *Norfolk* set sail, the trout arrived. They had been sent separately by Frank Buckland and Francis Francis. Both well-known naturalists and writers, as pioneers of modern fish culture in Britain Buckland and Francis were also rivals at a time when establishing non-native species overseas was all the rage (an activity on which biologists now look back in horror). In terms of boldly going where no trout had gone before, Australia was the big prize. It was a race neither wanted to lose. Numbering some 3,000 brown trout ova in total, Buckland's batch came from the river Itchen, near Winchester, and Francis's

The *Norfolk*, which ferried the first trout to Australia in 1864.

from two Thames tributaries, the Wey and the Wye.[5] Perhaps they left it to the last minute to try to catch each other out.

Youl, however, was known to be against sending trout to Australia. He was of the opinion that they grew faster than salmon, and feared the trout would devour their immature cousins in freshwater before they migrated to sea. But, Walker writes, 'when the trout eggs came to him at the dock and he realised all the pains that these gentlemen had been put to . . . he put them on board'. Youl marked the *Norfolk's* departure from London – on 21 January 1864 – with a letter to *The Times*:

> I feel confident your readers will most cordially join with me in wishing the good ship *Norfolk* a safe and speedy voyage, and in hoping that these precious little globules may retain their vitality in their damp mossy bed until they arrive at the sunny clime and golden shores of Australia.

The *Norfolk* dropped anchor in Melbourne on 15 April. 'With fear and trembling', a single box was opened. 'To the joy of anxious observers, it was found that the ova were in a sound and promising condition', Walker continues. The boxes were transferred to HMS *Victoria* for transport to Hobart and the Derwent river. Hobart's *Mercury* newspaper reported large crowds and flotillas of boats 'dressed in their gayest colours' that came to greet the new arrivals. No salute was fired for fear of mortally shocking the ova, Walker records, but 'ships dipped their ensigns as *Victoria* came up'. The 91-day journey was completed by a team of up to 50 men who hauled the boxes the final 4 miles (6.5 km) to Salmon Ponds hatchery on the Plenty river.[6]

The voyage was wasted on the salmon. Though some 30,000 ova survived the trip, and several thousand fish were successfully reared, once they headed to sea they were never seen again; not a single adult returned.[7] But the stowaway brown trout thrived in their new surroundings. From the remaining handful of 300 healthy eggs that had withstood the journey, the first southern hemisphere trout multiplied and spread. Distributed from Salmon Ponds by horse and cart, billycans and backpacks to rivers and lakes in Tasmania and beyond, they blazed the trail for the trout's globalization.

The faunal equivalent of afternoon tea or cricket to Englishmen abroad, trout were soon being ferried to such unlikely destinations as Ceylon, Kenya and Zululand. As one nineteenth-century British East Africa official put it, 'What white settlers will want to find here is wheat in their fields and trout in their rivers.'[8] The fish was now part of an ambitious programme of biological colonialism orchestrated by the acclimatization movement. Buckland, who had secured his trout a berth on the *Norfolk*, was a leading light of the movement, which emerged in Paris in the 1850s. (A man described as a walking zoo, Buckland, on returning to England from one overseas trip, was fined five shillings for smuggling a monkey on to a train. Told he needed a dog ticket for the monkey to travel, Buckland responded by pulling a large tortoise from his coat, and said, 'Perhaps you'll call that a dog, too?'[9]) Forming The Society for the Acclimatisation of Animals, Birds, Fishes, Insects and Vegetables within the UK in 1860, Buckland saw acclimatization as 'the art of discovering animals, beasts, birds, fishes, insects, plants and other natural products, and utilizing them in places where they were unknown before'.[10] Exotic animals such as the eland, ostrich, wallaby and zebra were imported to Europe, and familiar species

Salmon Ponds
hatchery, Tasmania,
c. 1870.

were sent abroad to recreate the agricultural, gastronomic and sporting opportunities of home. To this end, acclimatization societies proliferated.

The Acclimatisation Society of Victoria (closely involved in Youl's Tasmanian venture) in 1863 sent a wish list to the Foreign and Colonial Office in London that Noah himself might have penned.[11] Besides brown trout, they wanted salmon, char, grayling 'and other principal river fish of Europe', not to mention 'lobsters and crabs, and better kinds of fish of European seas' (what was wrong with Australia's aboriginal crustaceans and sea fishes, they did not say). British birds like the robin and hedge sparrow were 'desired in unlimited numbers' as 'farmers and gardeners suffer very much from the depredations of insects'. Woodpeckers were in urgent need because Australian trees were 'invested with very numerous larvae in the timber,

64

while in the whole country there is no representative of the wood-peckers appointed in other parts of the world to remedy this evil'. The importance attached to establishing trout in Australia is underlined by the number of regional acclimatization societies that sprang up dedicated solely to its introduction: in New South Wales alone there was the New England Trout Acclimatisation Society, the Central Acclimatisation Society, the Monaro Acclimatisation Society and the Orange Trout Acclimatisvation Society.[12]

Nicols praised the Australasian acclimatization societies for their energy and vision, and for leaving 'nothing undone to establish in the New World the most desirable animal colonists from the old'. Even if they made the odd mistake,

> and have introduced an unmitigated pest like the rabbit, they will one day find compensation in stalking the red deer and bringing the lordly salmon to grass among picturesque granitic hills, which may well recall to the eye of the sportsman many a wild scene in the highlands of bonnie Scotland.[13]

The new territories were seen as a kind of pristine, sporting Eden, where relocated game could be free of the human pollution and overcrowding of Europe. Nicols wrote:

> When even Scandinavia's pure waters have been tainted by civilisation, the sportsman will take his rifle and rod, and seek among the fern-covered ranges of the Australian Alps and the deep tarns and pools of Tasmania and New Zealand, the noble quarry which has found a congenial home at the Antipodes.[14]

THE MAIN TROUT POOL, FAIRY SPRINGS, ROTORUA, New Zealand. D.54

Postcard showing 'Fairy Springs' in Rotorua, New Zealand, teeming with trout.

And just as Europeans assumed themselves inherently superior to the dark-skinned peoples whose lands they invaded, they believed it only right and natural that European game fish should have dominion. If, Nicols said, 'distant and obscure' relatives of salmon and trout already inhabited rivers in India, New Zealand and the Falkland Islands, 'no one ignorant of anatomy would suspect the remotest connection of these impostors with the noble stock'.[15]

Impressive growth rates and sizes were attained by the newcomers down under. Nicols refers to tremendous trout in Tasmania, including 'a splendid fellow of over 16 lbs' taken on the Derwent river in 1874. The Antipodean trout 'outstripped their English ancestors in rapidity of growth, while retaining their excellence of flavour and beauty'.[16] Introduced to New

Zealand in 1868, the progeny of Salmon Ponds did so well there that they were sometimes mistaken for salmon (imported Pacific salmon, unlike their Atlantic counterparts, did take to the Southern Ocean). In 1884 Samuel Coleridge Farr, secretary of the North Canterbury Acclimatisation Society, landed a fish weighing 11.3 kg (25 lb) in the Waimakariri river. When it was shipped back to England for identification, experts at the Natural History Museum were surprised to discover it was a brown trout.[17] The species likewise took on greater dimensions on reaching Patagonia in the 1900s. The rivers of Tierra del Fuego in the far south were to gain a reputation among anglers for producing the largest sea-run trout on the planet.

The brown trout's colonization of North America dates from 1883, when a consignment of German eggs reached New York. Following the example of their human sponsors, the European settlers prospered in the land of opportunity. Swelled by reinforcements from Britain, the precocious brown trout was soon

Souvenir cover celebrating the centenary of the introduction of brown trout to New Zealand, 1967.

SOUVENIR COVER
To commemorate the centenary of the introduction of Brown Trout into New Zealand.

First Day of Issue: August 29th, 1967.

helping itself to rivers from Maine to the Rocky Mountains. The indigenous brook trout was muscled aside, writes Robert M. Poole. 'Brown trout grew bigger than brookies, could withstand warmer water and were fiercely territorial, sending their homegrown cousins scooting upstream in search of new quarters.'[18] Anglers were not overly enamoured of this warier, wilier import. A fishing report published in the *New York Times* in 1894 bemoans the 'unsolved problem' of how to catch the 'voracious European variety' that 'preys on the American trout'.[19] Specimens that weighed up to 4.5 kg (10 lb) had been recorded in New York State, 'but few are caught because ordinary trout tackle will not hold them', the correspondent adds. A recent skirmish ended with the trout 'breaking the angling wand in two places'.

Rainbow trout from North America followed a similar transoceanic trajectory. Americans, having adopted the brown trout, returned the favour, dispatching the species to Europe. More tolerant of warmer waters, the rainbow often picked up

Stocking of American rainbow trout in a reservoir in Kent, England, 1997.

where the brown left off. The fish can today be found in Costa Rican cloud forests, and in streams of the Ethiopian Highlands. 'Amazingly enough, more than 20 African nations have either naturally reproducing or artificially maintained rainbow trout populations', says Paul Schullery.[20] The fish has even infiltrated the capital of China: by 2002, the Beijing area had no less than 127 rainbow trout farms.[21] And in the city's northern Huairou district, the sought-after Western import has given rise to a popular visitor attraction known as the 'Beijing Trout Channel' (*Běijīng Hóng Zūn Yú Yi Tiáo Gōu*). 'A perennial favorite with visiting urbanites on weekends and holidays', the Trout Channel consists of dozens of fishing and barbecue spots set along a picturesque valley that draws one million tourists a year, according to the English-language paper *China Daily*.[22] Day-trippers come to drop baited hooks into ponds filled with luridly coloured rainbow trout that mill about like ornamental carp. It is an experience some local tour operators struggle to find words for:

Stamp marking the rainbow trout hatcheries in the former South African bantustan (or 'homeland') of Ciskei.

> Fishing the stocked tout [*sic*] is more of entertainment than of prefessional [*sic*] fishing . . . When you catch one or two trouts, the local people will weigh the fish. We will pay the fish [*sic*] and get the fish either roasted and sliced raw for your lunch – yummy!'

The Western concept of the trout as a noble game fish has evidently not always survived its cultural translocation.

In the southern New World, the rainbow beefed up and multiplied no less spectacularly than the brown. It may seem curious that trout took to the southern hemisphere as though they belonged there; however, the fact that they never colonized such countries as Argentina and New Zealand under their own steam was probably down to the barrier of the equatorial heat belt and the physical isolation of these regions (the reason, for example, why New Zealand has no native mammals except bats). Their success once humans acted as their travel agents can be explained by factors such as a lack of natural predators, parasites or competitors. 'They filled what seemed to be a true natural vacuum and, on balance, certainly contributed more to their new environment than they took away', argues Silvio Calabi.[23] Many would agree, not least the angling fraternity, but on a global scale this meddling is now seen as a major ecological mistake.

THE TROUT TURNS NASTY

The brown and rainbow trout make the top '100 of the World's Worst Invasive Alien Species', a list compiled by the World Conservation Union's (IUCN) Invasive Species Specialist Group.[24] Ranked with the likes of the domestic cat, black rat and zebra mussel, those 'precious globules' greeted so joyously in Tasmania grew into freshwater Genghis Khans. Inflicting heavy losses on Australian freshwater fauna, trout have eaten species of galaxiid fishes nearly to extinction. Though they are popular with Australian anglers, and said to be worth hundreds of millions of recreational dollars, many feel that the trout has outlasted its welcome. 'I can't understand why trout are treated differently from other imported predators, like foxes', a Victoria state MP told *The Australian* in 2004.[25] Environmentalists had taken to calling them 'spotted carp' (a coarse insult for a game fish), the paper added. In 2007, under the headline 'Trout Declared an "Alien Species"', the *Sunday Herald Sun* reported that the fish had been 'put on a hit-list for eradication' in southeastern Australia.[26] Efforts to save the barred galaxia, spotted tree frog, trout cod (no relation) and other at-risk species may necessitate the trout's removal.

Moving to the Falkland Islands, the South Atlantic outpost over which Britain went to war with Argentina in 1982, brown trout have been an occupying force since the 1950s. The zebra trout (not a trout, but another species named after its future nemesis) has all but disappeared from waters where the larger, aggressive invader occurs. Proposed measures to save the species – one of only two freshwater fishes indigenous to the Falklands – include brown trout exclusion zones in parts of the islands, enforced either by placing metal grills across streams and rivers, or electrofishing (whereby fish are temporarily stunned using an electric current, allowing the removal of undesirable species).[27]

The USA has been the major ecological battleground. While trout are domiciled there, in the west they plateaued out at around 2,000 m (6,560 ft) due to natural barriers like waterfalls. Extensive plantings at higher elevations opened up breathtaking new fishing areas, and introduced the trout to species that had never encountered them before. The highest-profile casualty is a frog which in the space of a decade 'has gone from obscurity to one of the most intensively-studied amphibians on Earth', according to US research biologist Roland Knapp.[28] The mountain yellow-legged frog, endemic to the Sierra Nevada range of California and Nevada, was once so common that during a wildlife survey in 1915 biologists could not help treading on them. Not much chance of squashing one today: more than 90 per cent of populations are gone.[29] While other threats have been implicated in their demise (not least the deadly chytrid fungus, a killer of amphibians globally), Knapp and fellow investigators are in no doubt about the main culprits. They date the start of the frog's decline to the 1950s, when fingerling trout were confettied over the Sierras from low-flying aircraft.

Anders Halverson likens the stocking of trout in post-war America to 'a full-scale military operation'.[30] Surplus military planes and pilots were redeployed after the Second World War in a new kind of aerial bombing campaign. A key early recruit was army training pilot Al Reese, who signed up with the California Department of Fish and Game. Reese's initial attempts – he tried dropping the fish in blocks of ice, and parachuting them in ice cream containers – were not a success. 'And so, one day, Reese and his assistants tried a simpler technique. They put fifty trout and some water in a five-gallon can and threw it out the window toward a hatchery pond about 350 feet below.'[31] The can missed, hitting rocks. 'But when observers recovered the twisted metal debris, they found sixteen fish still swimming in the small amount of water that remained.' To see if the fish could survive the airdrop without being in water, Reese and a colleague loaded some trout in a car and, driving at 70 miles per hour (112 kph), held them, one by one, out of the window for two minutes.[32] The fish mostly came through the ordeal okay.

Reese flew the first operational mission in July 1949. Ground staff saw the fish appear behind the plane like 'a cloud of mist' and hang for a moment in the sky, before they 'tumbled through the air in a spray of water and splashed like raindrops in the middle of the lake'. Within a year, Halverson says, California had 'shown the world what the future of fish stocking would look like'. (Buoyed by their success, the state began air-dropping other creatures – beavers, for example, which were outfitted with special parachutes.[33]) In 1953 alone it was reported that 'almost 3,000,000 baby trout rained down over 662 blue lakes in California's lofty Sierras'.[34] By the end of the 1950s, 'many other states were routinely using airplanes and helicopters to stock the backcountry. Thousands of previously fishless lakes were soon full of trout.'[35]

Mountain yellow-legged frogs, having thus far existed beyond the reach of aquatic predators, had no strategies for coping with trout. Sitting ducks, the trout gobbled them up. Official recognition of their plight finally came in 2007, when the IUCN listed the species as 'critically endangered'. Recent trout removal projects that recreate the frog's fishless environments have been

The release of millions of trout by aircraft over California's Sierra Nevada, from *Popular Mechanics* (1954).

A moment after the drop the water turns to mist and thousands of fingerling trout plunge toward the lake

It's Raining
BABY TROUT

By Claude M. Kreider

LAST SUMMER almost 3,000,000 baby trout "rained down" over 662 blue lakes in California's lofty Sierras.

This was not a miracle of nature brought about by the storm clouds hovering over

Aerial planting today does the job for $1.25 per thousand fish, and far more can be stocked during the short Sierra summer than could be planted with pack trains.

Experimental airplane stocking was first

73

'Planting trout by by air into Cascade lakes' in Oregon, advertisement, 1958.

judged a success.[36] The extent of its recovery will depend on how many of these unnatural trout waters the authorities decide to decommission.

It might appear to be a straight choice – trout or frog – but studies by Knapp in Yosemite National Park revealed the trout also had a profound negative impact on mountain snakes that eat the amphibians.[37] Meanwhile, in Japan, there is evidence of the alien trout's ecological tentacles stretching even further.[38] The victim, a species of forest spider, was caught in a domino chain flipped by the introduction of rainbow trout to the mountain streams of Hokkaido. Researchers found that the quick-rising trout deprived native char of more than 80 per cent of their diet, made up of terrestrial insects taken on the surface. This forced the char into grubbing on the river bottom for the larvae of aquatic insects for sustenance. In turn, this meant fewer river flies emerging as adults to be caught in the forest spiders' webs. As a result, spider numbers were down two-thirds.

THE TROUT LOSES ITS IDENTITY

Another unforeseen consequence of these transplants is that trout communities are becoming increasingly alike. Trout spread by humans are erasing local differences and endangering native strains. A symptom of our globalized age, scientists call this phenomenon biotic homogenization: 'virtually everything will live virtually everywhere, though the list of species that constitute "everything" will be small', writes David Quammen.[39] The trout vividly illustrates this process of biological impoverishment. In America, the brown trout, having squeezed out eastern brook trout, began doing the same to cutthroat trout in western states. The cutthroat was also out-competed by transplanted rainbow trout. Favoured because of its suitability for cultivation and sporting qualities, the rainbow carries an additional threat. Because rainbows and cutthroats are so closely related, what keeps them separate is geography – their natural ranges do not overlap. The rich kaleidoscope of cutthroat tribes is a product of their isolated watersheds; but when rainbows and cutthroats are put together, they do what comes naturally and hybridize. Variety is lost.

The westslope cutthroat of the northern Rocky Mountains may already have become irreversibly intimate with the rainbow. A 2009 study led by Clint Muhlfeld of the US Geological Survey

LOOKING FOR OUTDOOR FUN?

COME TO "UPSTATE, N.Y."
new market place of the world

There's outdoor fun in abundance here — fishing, skiing, hunting, boating and more. Famous Upstate, N.Y., parks, many resorts, countless lakes, rivers and streams make this a fine place to visit, a fine place to locate a plant.

Here, surrounded by the rich markets of the northeast and Canada, you'll find plentiful Niagara Mohawk power, excellent transportation, a stable supply of skilled labor, and an educational system second to none. We have a confidential and complete plant location service, including a detailed inventory of buildings and sites, and market information. For full information write Director of Area Development, Niagara Mohawk, Dept. N-49, Syracuse 2, N.Y.

POWERED BY

NIAGARA

MOHAWK

found that first generation hybrids, or 'cutbows', were more fecund than pure-breds.[40] Inheriting the rainbow's stronger migration instinct, cutbows also travelled further, accelerating the cutthroat's loss of identity. The study suggests that only five to ten per cent of westslope cutthroat populations remain untainted, and that the rest are too far gone to be preserved. 'You can't un-hybridize them . . . and the horse has been out of the barn quite a long time', commented study co-author Fred Allendorf.[41] The Alvord cutthroat of Oregon may have already interbred into extinction (mountain searches continue for remnant, pure-bred survivors). Others affected include rainbow relatives the golden trout, redband trout and Gila trout. This muddying into sameness is also happening among European trout. Cultivated brown trout used to replenish or 'improve' fishing waters are typically of Atlantic, northern European stock. Dumped by the tank load, they have encroached on other strains, particularly Mediterranean and Adriatic lineages. Consequently, many wild

A 1959 promotional campaign for upstate New York recruits rainbow trout to sell the region's outdoor attractions.

A native cutthroat trout, western Montana.

The town of Gore, South Island, New Zealand, welcomes visitors with a sculpture of a giant brown trout.

populations, including those classed as separate species, such as the striking marble trout, are imperilled.[42]

The threat from standardized trout communities goes much deeper than aesthetics. The wild trout's manifold beauties are an expression of genetic diversity. Perfected over millennia, each population is individually tailored to its locality. Homogenization risks destroying the gene bank their existence is founded on. Michael Hansen, head of the Department of Biological Science at the University of Aarhus, Denmark, speaking in 2005, said studies show that 'cultivated salmonids have different properties as compared to wild salmonids, for instance in terms of reduced shyness, increased growth rate, higher aggression levels in juveniles; but poor performance of adult spawners, reduced egg size, etc. – all factors that are important for survival in the wild'.[43]

'We are reducing the genetic resources of wild populations', Hansen added. 'Genetic variation [allows] populations and species to adapt to future environmental changes. It is unfortunate that genetic variation is eroded when at the same time global warming and other environmental changes due to human influences make it even more important that populations have the "building blocks" to adapt.'

So, yes, a big ecological mistake – one which government agencies are trying to remedy where not too late, through removing or banning non-native trout. But it is hard not to relate to – admire, even – this incredible fish saga. Poole, an American, sees the modern story of trout in his country as 'a fair reflection of our own restless history, with its marathon migrations, its paroxysms of prejudice, its well-intentioned blunders and its reassuring urge to set those blunders right again'.[44] As for the formerly troutless southern lands it conquered, Schullery imagines the surprise of those 'earnest visionaries' who took the fish there if they knew today that people object to what they did. 'What could be wrong in ensuring the survival of these beautiful animals in some remote corners of the earth? And besides that, what could possibly be wrong with redefining the earth as Planet Trout?'[45]

4 Filleted Trout

In a healthy living guide of 1584, *The Haven of Health*, Tudor physician Thomas Cogan describes the trout as 'so sound in nourishing, that when we would saie in English, that a man is throughly sound, we use to say that he is sound as a Troute'. The old saying survives, as does the trout's reputation for wholesomeness. Marketed as a healthy food, it is low in fat yet rich in fatty acids, which are said to guard against heart disease and promote mental wellbeing. A measure of our fondness for its tasty meat was the trout's rapid domestication in the nineteenth century. In becoming the first mass-produced fish, it triggered a revolution in world food production, evidenced by today's multi-billion-dollar fish-farming industry.

The *truht* or *sceot*, as it was called in Old English (the Anglo-Saxon *sceot* also meant 'shot' or 'to shoot', a word that well describes a startled trout's darting motion) has long been a staple of British cuisine. *The British Museum Cookbook* (1995) gives an Anglo-Saxon recipe for griddled trout, seasoned with herbs available in tenth-century East Anglia: mint, sage, rosemary and thyme.[1] The fifteenth-century *A Treatyse of Fysshynge Wyth an Angle* praised the trout as a 'ryght deyntous fysshe',[2] and Izaak Walton wrote that 'the most dainty palates have allowed precedency to him'.[3]

Thomas Barker, a fancy chef who wrote on fishing at the same time as Walton, seems to have had a culinary obsession

Gustave Courbet,
The Trout, 1873,
oil on canvas.

with the fish. He describes preparing 'a great Dish of Trouts', with, to begin with, 'Trouts in broth, which is restorative: Trouts broyled, cut and filled with sweet Herbes chopt: Trouts calvored hot with Antchovaes sauce: Trouts boyled; out of which Kettle I make three Dishes; the one for a Soused Dish, another for a Stew'd Dish, the third for a hot Dish.' And for the main course: 'Trouts calvored cold: Trouts flat cold: Baked Trouts: Trouts marilled, that will eat perfect and sweet three moneths in the heat of Summer.' Barker, who claimed to have cooked in 'most Ambassadors Kitchins', does not confine himself to English trout recipes:

> The Italian he stewes upon a Chafing-dish of coals, with white Wine, Cloves, and Mace, Nutmegs sliced, a little Ginger: you must understand when this fish is stewed, the same liquor that the fish is stewed in, must be beaten with some Butter and the juyce of a Lemmon, before it is dish'd for the service. The French doe add to this a slice or two of Bacon.[4]

Charles Cotton, Walton's fishing companion and writing collaborator,[5] gave this advice:

Take your trout, wash, and dry him with a clean napkin; then open him, and having taken out his guts, and all the blood, wipe him very clean within, but wash him not; and give him three scotches with a knife to the bone, on one side only. After which take a clean kettle, and put in as much hard stale beer (but it must not be dead), vinegar, and a little white wine, and water, as will cover the fish you intend to boil: then throw into the liquor a good quantity of salt, the rind of a lemon, a handful of sliced horse-radish-root, with a handsome little fagot of rosemary, thyme, and winter-savory. Then set your kettle upon a quick fire of wood.[6]

Cotton stresses that trout should be eaten fresh, 'within four or five hours after he be taken'.

Trout are typically eaten grilled, fried, poached or cooked *en papillote* (in paper or aluminium foil). A signature method is *truite au bleu*, which involves dousing small, freshly killed trout with vinegar and putting them in boiling water. The effect of the vinegar on the mucus coating the fish is to turn it blue.[7] Yet the trout's days as a luxury food of the kind Thomas Barker served up are probably over. With modern aquaculture and the proliferation of heavily stocked put-and-take fisheries (usually artificial lakes or ponds), the trout has become an everyday foodstuff. It stares dolefully from supermarket shelves and anglers' freezers, which are often poorly disguised fish mortuaries due to the build-up of uneaten corpses. The problem of surplus trout and jaded palates is countered with endless new recipes. There are 100 to choose from in Patricia Ann Hayes's *The Trout Cook*, which, says its jacket, 'offers a source of fresh inspiration for every cook seeking new ways with trout'.[8] Suggestions include trout versions of rollmop herrings, beef Wellington, kedgeree (replacing haddock), lasagne, ratatouille and shepherd's pie. Reinvented as the humble trout, the fish has become an all-purpose ingredient.

A dish the book omits is *rakørret*, or fermented trout. Peculiar to Norway, it is an experience that visitors who get within smelling distance are unlikely to forget. 'Something, to misquote Hamlet, is rotten in the state of Norway', wrote one British journalist, after a trip to Oslo.[9] 'I've eaten fried snakes in the wilds of Chinese Wuyishan and even looked a braised Faroese puffin

William Walls, *Trout and Eels on a Bankside*, 1915, oil on canvas.

Trout prepared for fermenting to make *rakørret*.

in its reproachful eye, all in the course of duty. At *rakørret*, how-ever, I draw the line.' Tasting better than it smells, with a flavour not unlike that of a 'high', gooey cheese, the putrefied fish is a winter delicacy, to be enjoyed with family and friends.[10] A tradi-tional dish dating back to medieval times, *rakørret* is raw trout that has been fermented at about 4°C (39°F) for anything up to a year. In the past, fish were buried or stored in underground cel-lars, providing a vital if risky source of protein during the harsh Scandinavian winter, but today plastic buckets are used. The trout are gutted, coated in a mix of salt and sugar, then covered in brine. Weights are placed on the lid of the bucket, keeping the fish tightly packed. Because of the lack of oxygen, they fer-ment without decomposing (there is a slight danger of botulism if strict hygiene rules are not adhered to). Norwegian food writer Andreas Viestad says:

Enzymes from microorganisms transform the long protein molecules, and lactic acid bacteria break down the carbohydrates. That is similar to cheesemaking, and the result can be as odiferous as the Frenchest of cheeses, and with a soft texture; in extreme cases, the fish flesh is so soft you can spread it. As with cheese made with unpasteurized milk, some risk is involved, but also great rewards for those who know how to appreciate the outcome.[11]

The outcome was not so good in *Las Truchas* (Trout), a Spanish film directed by José Luis García Sánchez that won best movie at the Berlin Film Festival in 1978. The trout of his allegorical satire about life under General Franco are eaten by members of a fishing club at their annual dinner. The trout are rotten because something, to borrow an earlier misquote, is rotten in the state of Spain. The middle-class club members pretend that, despite the awful taste, the trout are fine. They carry on as normal, eating, making speeches and giving awards, as, one by one, they keel over, mortally poisoned.

CULTIVATED TROUT

The origins of cultivated trout are traced to the Romans. They were known to have a penchant for the fish, not least, according to Harry E. Wedeck's *Dictionary of Aphrodisiacs*, after lovemaking: 'Roman matrons, sexually exhausted, were fond of trout caught in a little stream in the Vosges Mountains.'[12] Rising in the Vosges, in what was then northern Gaul, is the Moselle, a river that was renowned for producing the finest trout.[13] (The poet Ausonius refers to the fish, 'whose back is starred with purple spots', in his tribute to the river, *Mosella*, composed in AD 370.) The Romans also gathered live fish for growing for the table in purpose-built ponds or *dulces*. Though classical authors say little about the species they kept, perhaps the earliest recorded keeper of trout was the notorious emperor Nero (*r.* AD 54–68). The ruins of his splendid villa near Subiaco in the Apennine mountains overlook the Aniene river, where Nero built the highest dams known in the Roman world.[14] 'By damming [the river] three times, with dams more than two hundred feet high, he created three mountain lakes, where he could indulge in the sport of trout fishing and in cold bathing', wrote the Roman archaeologist Rodolfo Lanciani.[15] Thanks to this massive feat of engineering, Nero enjoyed his own personal supply of trout, which the emperor is said to have caught in a net made of gold.[16]

Roman fish ponds spread to other parts of the empire, where their remains have been unearthed next to those of Roman villas. An intriguing English example is Shakenoak in Oxfordshire; archaeologists suspect that the site's arrangement of stone-walled ponds and connecting streams may indicate the presence of an ancient, second-century trout farm.

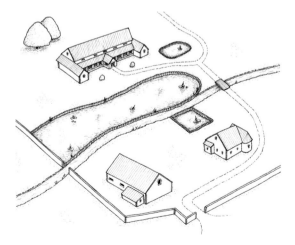

Joseph Wilkins, a possible Roman trout farm excavated at Shakenoak, Oxfordshire, England.

Here not one, but three ponds were found close to the brook running through the complex of villa buildings . . . Pond 1, with its running water supply, is interpreted as a breeding tank, whilst the isolated Pond 3, being close to a metalled roadway, is seen as a holding tank for fish awaiting shipment to market.[17]

The ponds imply a sophisticated level of aquaculture, say researchers, 'the most likely occupants being trout'.[18] Situated on the edge of the limestone Cotswold Hills, an area laced with spring-fed trout streams, the location would indeed seem well chosen for such an enterprise.

In general, however, the trout's exacting living requirements of cool, well-oxygenated waters and gravel streams for breeding did not recommend it for fishpond husbandry. Medieval fishponds nearly always held coarse fish: carp and bream mainly, but also eel, perch, pike and tench. John Taverner, in his wonderfully titled *Certaine Experiments Concerning Fish and Fruite* (1600), talks about the difficulties of keeping trout.[19] Besides their inability to 'spawne in any standing poole', if 'the water commeth any thing neare the mud, your Troughts will then die'. And, he warns, 'they must be very charily [carefully] handled in the cariage, and a few of them caried in a great deale of faire and cleane water, and that in cold weather, and may not be handled with hands, but in a hand-net very charily' (unlike the carp, a robust fish that can cope with being out of water for relatively long periods). Taverner says ponds of less than 5 acres (2 hectares) are too small for trout, advising instead 'ten or twelve acres of ground or more, neare any river where Troughts are', with 'good store of small fry to feede on', but no pike.

The secret to cultivating trout (and salmon) is to breed them artificially – an innovation widely credited to a fifteenth-century

French monk named Dom Pinchon. If genuinely his discovery (the supposed source is a now elusive manuscript from 1420), it would represent the earliest recorded description of the artificial propagation of any fish, marking a watershed in the history of aquaculture.[20] Based at Réome Abbey in Burgundy, Dom Pinchon's investigations were doubtless inspired by the dietary strictures of his religion, which forbade the consumption of meat from four-legged animals on Fridays and other days of abstinence. A reliable supply of fresh trout would have been a blessing, if only to keep muddy-tasting pond carp off the refectory menu. The monk is said to have bred the fish using wooden boxes that had wickerwork ends to allow water to flow over the fertilized eggs, which were deposited in the bottom and covered in sand.[21] Herbert Spencer Davis, writing in the 1950s, said: 'there are still some doubting Thomases who believe that he used trout eggs that had been spawned naturally. However that may be, there appears to be no question that he was the first to use a hatching box involving modern principles.'[22]

The technique was rediscovered independently in the 1750s by Stephan Ludwig Jacobi, a wealthy German landowner. Concerned about a steep decline in trout numbers in a stream on his Westphalian estate, Jacobi took charge of their reproduction by stripping the ripe hen and cock fish of their eggs and milt, then mixing the two in containers of water. Once fertilized, the eggs were buried in gravel inside a long oaken box with fine gratings over the top and ends. 'The box was then anchored in a stream with clear running water, and the incubation of the eggs was left to nature', writes Davis. 'A number of fish farms were established, and the business prospered for a time.'[23] So impressed was Britain's King George III (a fellow German by blood, he was concurrently Duke of Brunswick-Lüneburg and Prince Elector of Hanover) that Jacobi was awarded a medal and

The Kalletal region of Germany, which produces this schnapps, has the trout as its emblem, in honour of fish-farming pioneer Stephan Ludwig Jacobi.

a pension for life. Yet the royal endorsement of a king who was already succumbing to his debilitating madness might not have been the best publicity, suggests environmental historian Darin Kinsey.[24] In any case, scientific institutions at home and abroad failed either to believe or investigate Jacobi's techniques. 'They have considered this method of artificial breeding of trouts and salmon as a false chimera', Jacobi complained.[25] 'His methods were soon forgotten', says Davis, 'and little was heard of fish culture for nearly a hundred years'.[26]

FACTORY TROUT

Trout would once again be the catalysts for the fish culture breakthrough, leading this time to an aquatic revolution in food production. Its unlikely instigators were two French peasants,

Joseph Remy and Antoine Géhin, who scraped a living catching trout in the Vosges Mountains mentioned earlier.

> Although uneducated and ignorant, they became alarmed at the rapid disappearance of trout in their favorite streams and spent much time in a study of their habits, especially during the spawning season . . . in one instance during a full moon they kept a school of trout constantly in view for four consecutive days and nights. The result was the rediscovery of the methods of Jacobi.[27]

The great advantage of 'artificial fecundation', as it was known, was that the majority of each female's thousands of eggs (a trout produces roughly 2,000 ova per kilogram of body-weight) could be successfully raised into fry; whereas only a tiny fraction of wild-born offspring survive predators, disease and impacts such as droughts or floods. Even so, it was not until 1848, five years after Remy and Géhin had reported their re-stocking operations to officials, that Parisian scientists, having previously dismissed the pair as country bumpkins, took notice. That there was another revolution in France that same year, when the last French king, Louis-Philippe I, fled to England (it is said he travelled in disguise under the name 'Mr Smith'), was not a coincidence, according to Kinsey.[28] Food shortages had been a major cause of peasant unrest, and the new republic's first president, Napoleon III, came to power on a platform that promised 'not only to ensure an unchecked food supply for the people, but also to democratize the same kinds of "exotic" foods available to the aristocracy'.[29] There was also a 'growing democratization of science that manifested itself in the nation's Sociétés d'Émulation'.[30] These local science clubs, which sprang up in the provinces, were more inclined to show an interest in rustic innovators like Remy and Géhin than were the distant academic elite.

The two fishermen each received a pension and a state-licensed tobacco shop to run – then a not unusual expression of state gratitude to common citizens. The younger Géhin was also paid to travel around the country, promoting artificial fecundation to the masses. Meanwhile, in 1852, a government research station was constructed at Huningue in Alsace, northeastern France, to develop the pair's breeding procedures. Headed by fisheries scientist Victor Coste, the state-of-the-art complex included indoor rearing ponds, mechanized water lifts and 24-hour security. It was dubbed the *'piscifactoire'* – and with it the factory fish was born. 'Just as in our grand manufactories, we will be able to infinitely multiply [fish] for distribution at the lowest price of consumption', proclaimed one commentator.[31] In a bullish progress report, Coste stated: 'There is no branch of industry or husbandry, which, with less chance of loss, offers an easier certainty of profit.'[32] A study estimated that fish from the *piscifactoire* production line could increase revenues from France's freshwater fisheries from six million francs to in excess of 900 million francs within four years.[33] If this was overestimating Huningue's fish-generating capabilities, by 1860 the facility had nevertheless churned out more than 100 million trout and salmon eggs for distribution across France and beyond.[34]

Humans spent millennia domesticating livestock like cattle and sheep, yet here was a food animal that could be tamed in a single generation. Offspring of fish 'gathered on the shores of lakes in Switzerland, the Rhine, and the Danube . . . now live like perfectly submissive barnyard animals', Coste marvelled.[35] Emboldened by initial results, he is said to have promised every Frenchman 'a daily giant trout, in the same manner as Henry IV had promised every English farmer a chicken a week'.[36] Other

'Experimenting Ponds at the Huningue Fish Nurseries', Alsace, France, from *The Illustrated London News* (1864).

species were added to the aquaculture trials, and Coste successfully carried out experiments to create fish hybrids (though an attempt at crossing trout with pike presumably failed). Huningue became a source of French national pride: 'It is in our country that fish culture has grown, has been perfected, and has finally come to constitute an actual branch of industry', wrote naturalist Jules Haime.[37] His boast was, if anything, an understatement, says Kinsey.

> Aquatic resources would no longer simply be harvested; they would be manufactured and reinvented so that by kind and abundance they would be superior to the raw material provided by nature. Grafted to a larger imperial ethos, aquaculture as an idea spread rapidly from the French epicenter to far-flung global peripheries.[38]

France invented the factory trout, but it did not become its leading producer. Following its crushing defeat in the Franco–Prussian War (1870–71), France lost the enterprise's imperial sponsor, Napoleon III, and ceded its famous fish factory to Germany (along with Alsace and Lorraine). The newly created German Empire took up where France left off in Europe; meanwhile, across the Atlantic, the USA was poised to launch its secret weapon: the rainbow trout.

The story of the rainbow's rise to dominance is told by Anders Halverson in *An Entirely Synthetic Fish* (2010), a book subtitled *How Rainbow Trout Beguiled America and Overran the World*. A bold claim to make for a fish, but the claim stacks up: on restaurant menus and in supermarkets, the rainbow trout is a rival to the ubiquitous farmed salmon. In 2007 some 590,000 tons of farmed rainbow trout with a value in excess of $2.5 billion were harvested worldwide.[39] In countries of the European Union, the fish is the leading aquaculture species along with the blue mussel; unlike the marine mollusc, however, the rainbow is not native to Europe. In 2008 the US reared more than 24 million kg (53 million lb) of trout, overwhelmingly rainbows,

Early fish propagation equipment of the type used at Huningue, from Auguste Jourdier, *La Pisciculture et la Production des Sangsues* (1856).

A female trout being stripped of its eggs, from Auguste Jourdier, *La Pisciculture et la Production des Sangsues*.

Trout propagators 'strip' an adult fish, United States, 19th century.

for food and recreational use.[40] The rapid geographical expansion of the species is also extraordinary. In the latter half of the nineteenth century it was still restricted to westernmost North America and the easternmost tip of Russia; by the dawn of the twenty-first century it had infiltrated at least 80 countries on every continent except Antarctica.[41]

The rainbow was the natural replacement for the European brown trout when the new fish culture technology came to the States. The American Fish Culturists' Association, founded in 1870 with the aim of reinvigorating the country's degraded

94

fisheries, quickly proved an effective lobbyist for artificial fish propagation. Crucially, the group won federal backing for a nationwide programme of fish stocking and, in 1871, President Ulysses S. Grant signed into law a bill that formed the United States Fish Commission (USFC). Fish culture in America, especially the culture of trout, was now government policy. In deploying rainbow trout and other fish (freshwater bass, eels, perch, pike, shad) around the country, the USFC harnessed that great motor for the development and industrialization of America: the railroad. The pilgrim fathers of the fish that 'overran the world' embarked from California for New York in the spring of 1875 – 'the first time rainbow trout had been shipped out of their native range'.[42] The USFC developed customized carriages equipped with water tanks, refrigeration and aeration systems for ferrying their aquatic passengers; sleeping and dining quarters for fisheries staff were also provided. These fish carriages crisscrossed North America, delivering live fry and ova, until 1947.[43]

As for why the rainbow became the number one hatchery trout – as opposed, say, to the brown or cutthroat trout – one key

A shoal of hatchery-raised rainbow trout.

Front cover of
The New Yorker
(18 April 1953)
depicting anglers
awaiting the
hatchery trout
delivery truck.

reason was its suitability as an introduced game fish. It is able to withstand a greater water temperature range – 0 to 27c° (32 to 81°F) – than its peers, and its sporting qualities made it a favourite with anglers. 'We know of no better game fish', remarked Theodore Gordon. 'It leaps again and again when hooked, and rushes madly down stream.'[44] Also, from a farming standpoint, the rainbow copes well with the stresses of living in captivity and, clinchingly, it is the fastest-growing trout species.

Trout farming from the outset was primarily a means for replenishing rivers and lakes, and stocking waters where trout had not existed before, but following the Second World War the

The Wisconsin
Conservation
Commission
makes a rail
delivery of trout
fry, 1921.

A custom-built
American 'fish car'
used for ferrying
live trout, 1916.

★ April 18, 1953

THE

Price 20 cents

NEW YORKER

A state-run trout hatchery in Michigan, 1957.

emphasis shifted to food production. The ravages of war left Western Europe hungry and rationed, and on the lookout for new, intensive farming methods to maximize yields. The cultivated trout was an obvious candidate. Besides its capacity for mass production, there was an assured market for a fish whose culinary stock had risen since its association with the gentlemanly art of fly-fishing. In England, where the trout was nurtured and preserved for the sporting enjoyment of the ruling classes, it had an aura of refinement and exclusivity. The trout, Mrs Beeton wrote in her best-selling *Book of Household Management* (1861), is 'esteemed by the moderns for its delicacy'. Conversely, the once prized and eminently farmable carp, eulogized by Izaak Walton as 'the queen of rivers', had sunk to the status of 'coarse' fish, which in Britain means practically inedible. Today the UK is one of the major trout-farming nations (others include Chile, Denmark, France, Germany, Iran, Italy, Norway and Spain).

Trout fry are raised in circular tanks with a supply of clean, well-oxygenated river or spring water that circulates to form a central vortex where waste accumulates for easy removal.[45] Once

98

the fry reach 8–10 cm (3–4 in) in length, they are transferred to concrete raceways, ponds with continuously flowing water, or floating cages in lakes or at sea (an option favoured in colder regions like Canada and Scandinavia where freshwater is liable to freeze over in winter). Cage systems measuring 6 m (20 ft) wide and 5 m (16 ft) deep may contain up to 100,000 fish; densities can reach the equivalent of 80 450-g (1-lb) trout per square metre of water surface.

Crammed in like proverbial sardines, farm trout are prone to an ungodly array of diseases and parasites. On its website, the Food and Agriculture Organization of the United Nations lists fourteen to watch out for.[46] They include furunculosis (bacterial infection) – 'inflammation of intestine, reddening of fins, boils on body, pectoral fins infected, tissues die back'. Vibriosis (bacterial) – 'loss of appetite, fins and areas around vent and mouth become reddened, sometimes bleeding around mouth and gills, potential high mortality'. Infective Pancreatic Necrosis (viral) – 'erratic swimming, eventually to bottom of tank where death occurs'. Viral Haemorrhagic Septicaemia – 'bulging eyes and, in some cases, bleeding eyes, pale gills, swollen abdomen, lethargy'. Whirling Disease (parasitic) – 'darkening of skin, swimming in spinning fashion, deformities around gills and tail fin, death eventually occurs'. Hexamitaisis Octomitis (parasitic) – 'lethargic, sinking to bottom of tank where death occurs, some fish make sudden random movements'. Preventing the trout from turning belly up hence entails a regulated arsenal of drugs and chemicals.

Fed either by hand or automatic feeders, the fish are grown on high-energy pellets made from fish meal, fish oil, cereals and, increasingly, protein-packed alternatives to fish such as soybeans. To replicate the pinkness of flesh consumers expect of salmon and trout (a colour that in wild trout derives from a diet of carotenoid-rich crustaceans, particularly freshwater shrimp), the pigments astaxanthin or canthaxanthin are added. Modern-day fish farms employ machines that help to check and sort the trout throughout their production cycle – to eliminate the deceased, diseased or otherwise defective, and to grade the fish, so that when they finally drop off the conveyor belt they are uniform in size.

MODIFIED TROUT

Domestication has altered the trout's biology as radically as its lifestyle. Next to the untamed fish, the farm version is barely

recognizable. Already by 1939, the US government's head of fish culture anticipated the creation of 'an entirely "synthetic" fish'.[47] Hatchery rainbows were the subject of artificial selection programmes that collected desirable traits from natural populations and propagated them in cultivated strains. 'Rainbows have been bred to grow faster, mature earlier, and breed at different times of the year. Culturists have tried to select for disease resistance, fecundity, and even such things as color, shape, and fighting ability', Halverson writes.[48]

The fish's modification by humans goes deeper than that. Farm trout have even lost their sexes and the ability to procreate. Because female trout grow faster than males, unisex stock is manufactured by fertilizing eggs with sperm from masculinized females (females that are given hormones to make them grow testes). The offspring are then rendered infertile by converting them into 'triploids' – fish with three female sex chromosomes (XXX) instead of the normal two (XX). This is achieved by subjecting the fertilized eggs to heat or pressure treatment. Lacking mature sex organs or a mating season, all-female triploids devote their interrupted energies to piling on weight and improving output. They do not lose their desirable pinkness to egg production, which utilizes the red pigment in their meat. Having an extra set of chromosomes causes other innate differences: triploids have fewer but larger cells in their organs and tissues, including the brain, liver, kidney and the flesh itself.[49] In short, it is not the same fish.

Perhaps surprisingly given their modified status, triploids have received the green light for release into the wild for the purpose of conservation. In 2008 the UK's Environment Agency announced that from 2015 the estimated 750,000 trout stocked annually in rivers and lakes in England and Wales must be triploid-only.[50] Because triploids are sterile, they are seen as a

A large triploid trout.

solution to the problem of farm trout interbreeding with threatened wild populations. Some critics, however, argue that because the non-breeders eat more and grow bigger, they may do more harm than good by outcompeting native trout.

Bananas are triploids, and we eat them without any fuss, so triploid fish are probably nothing to lose our appetites over. But the prospect of transgenic trout may be harder to swallow. Accompanied by inevitable media cries of 'Frankenfish!', their development involves inserting genetic material appropriated from other organisms. 'Meet Arnie, the Terminator Trout with the Physique of a Body-builder' is how the *Daily Mail* headlined the unveiling of one such creation in 2010.[51] 'Arnie', a horribly misshapen rainbow trout, owed his 'bulging shoulders' and 'six-pack abs' to a dose of cattle-type DNA. The fish carries a mutated gene found in Belgian blue cattle (a breed noted for its 'double muscled' appearance), which inhibits myostatin, a protein that slows muscle growth.[52] The quite literally beefed-up trout grows 15 to 20 per cent more flesh than standard trout, and has 'significant implications for commercial aquaculture', says Arnie's creator, a professor of fisheries and aquaculture at the University of Rhode Island.

Other GM trout have been engineered to produce human growth hormone, or have had their growth hormones permanently switched on, or carry antifreeze genes from Arctic fishes so they can be farmed in waters that would otherwise be too cold. Fredrik Sundström from the University of Gothenburg, Sweden, warns of the ecological consequences if these fish were to escape. His studies with trout and salmon indicate that larger-growing, disease-resistant transgenics could outmuscle resident fauna and spread manmade genes to wild trout. 'Under certain conditions transgenic fish do better than the wild types', he says. 'Most likely they would be able to spawn in nature. If they escape and interbreed you would have the same kind of fish in nature with the transgene.'[53] Transgenic trout might be swimming against a tide of uneasiness and suspicion towards GM foods, but it is probably only a matter of time before they make it on to our dinner plates.[54]

Farmed trout are supplied either fresh (with a shelf life of up to two weeks if kept on ice) or frozen as gutted fish or fillets.

'Arnie, the Terminator Trout' – a transgenic trout unveiled by scientists in 2010.

Also sold smoked, cooked and tinned, the fish's potential health benefits as a rich source of omega-3 fatty acids include protection against coronary heart disease, relief from the symptoms of rheumatoid arthritis and a reduced risk of depression and other diseases linked to abnormal cognitive function, according to findings compiled by the British Trout Association. The industry body also commissioned its own research, which went so far as to suggest that, because of a decline in the consumption of oily fish, human evolution 'is in danger of going into reverse'.[55] 'Professor [Michael] Crawford, director of the Institute of Brain Chemistry and Human Nutrition at London Metropolitan University, claims that a fish diet was responsible for the rise of *Homo sapiens* from the evolutionary swamp. "A diet of fish containing omega-3 was essential for the necessary cerebral expansion which transformed our predecessors . . . We need to get back to feeding our minds as well as our bodies, otherwise the future of the nation is grim."'[56]

While the farmed trout offers a healthy substitute for oily marine fishes that have been depleted by overfishing, it is not to everybody's taste. *The World Encyclopedia of Food* states: 'The flavor of [trout] raised in captivity does not come near to matching that of the wild variety . . . French food critics have likened the tame trout to "a wet bandage," and called it, "a cotton-fleshed substitute."'[57] British celebrity chef Hugh Fearnley-Whittingstall

has this simple buying advice: 'Don't' – 'Farmed trout, which are sure to be rainbows, are almost without exception disappointingly insipid and unpleasantly muddy.'[58]

Sound as a trout? Not judging from today's chemically dependent, genetically altered, artificially coloured, sex-changed, sterile, misshapen, cage-worn factory version. Thanks to our meddling, the trout is not as sound as before.

5 Desirable Trout

'One of the most fascinating things about trout is the way they fascinate men', wrote the great poet Ted Hughes. 'Why have so few women confessed to this weakness in writing? . . . Do they ever feel that weird, ghostly kiss at the glimpse, even at the thought, of a trout, as so many men do?'[1] In confessing this weakness, the trout's male literary admirers have marked the fish out. 'About no other species has such a wealth of writing accumulated, some of it the most beautiful and memorable in angling literature', state Fred Buller and Hugh Falkus.[2] 'We find ourselves enthralled with the quicksilver poetry of the fish', says Ernest Schwiebert, an American exponent of the genre.[3] For Hughes, 'the trout belongs to some special privileged order of creation. They are like the beautiful girl in the school.'[4] Trout: the wild's freckled Lolita, pure, innocent, beautiful. A ravishing prize, and one that is all too easily lost.

CASTING FOR TROUT

Scholars of angling trace fishing for trout with artificial flies back to Roman times. Aelian (Claudius Aelianus) records in his natural history guide to the ancient world of circa AD 200, *On the Nature of Animals*, that Macedonians cast with rods to 'fish with speckled skins'.[5] 'They fasten red wool around a hook, and

fix onto the wool two feathers which grow under a cock's wattles, and which in colour are like wax.' Even in this earliest unambiguous description of fly-fishing, Aelian well captures the trout's allure: 'Coming up by its shadow, it opens its mouth gently and gulps down the fly.'

'The Macedonian fly must be the most interesting fly of all time', says fly-fishing historian Andrew Herd.[6] Representing (fisher)man's evolutionary leap from bait angler to artful imitator of nature, the fly's appearance and the insect it represented have been the subject of 'an immense amount of speculation'.[7] Reconstructions place the two cock neck hackles down each side of the wool body, or wound around it for a 'palmered', bottle-brush effect, while Herd speculates that the fly mimicked 'the large and delicate *Siphlonurus* species of mayfly seen in southern European summers'.[8] (The early summer insect called 'the mayfly' in Britain and Ireland is just one of various mayflies, or *Ephemeroptera*, important to trout. Here we shall differentiate by titling the former 'Mayfly'.)

As there is little to glean from the Middle Ages about trout fishing, let us skip to the age of the printing press and the fifteenth-century information revolution. Wynkyn de Worde, having served as apprentice to William Caxton, the first printer of English, made his name as the publisher of Britain's newest craze: books. In 1496 he bundled a 'lytell paunflet' on angling,

A Treatyse of Fysshynge Wyth an Angle, in with an edition of hunting essays, *The Boke of St Albans*. An instant bestseller, it went through ten editions in four years. Though authorship of the *Treatyse* (as the text is simply and affectionately known), written in about 1450, is far from certain, it is popularly attributed to an English nun, Juliana Berners, prioress of Sopwell Priory in Hertfordshire. Modern angling writers (nearly all male, predictably) doubt that this seminal work was really hers. David Profumo, writing in the *Daily Telegraph* in the 500th anniversary year of the publication of the *Treatyse* in 1996, said, 'In the absence of other contenders her legend persists, making her one of our rare female authors on the subject. Personally, I think it's the work of a bloke.'

Besides tips on line strength – nine horsetail hairs for average-sized trout, twelve hairs for bigger ones – and baits – 'the grub under the cow turd' is recommended for May – a section is given

Frontispiece to *A Treatyse of Fysshynge Wyth an Angle* (1496), the earliest known printed work on fly-fishing in English.

to twelve seasonal fly patterns for trout and grayling. Killing in July is the 'waspe flye': 'body of blacke wull & lappid abowte wt yelow threde: the winges of the bosarde [buzzard]'; and for August, the 'drake flye': 'body of blacke wull & lappyd abowte wyth blacke sylke: wynges of the mayle of the blacke drake wyth a blacke heed'.[9] Piscatorial scribes faithfully reproduced the flies of the *Treatyse*, dubbed the 'Jury of Twelve', for more than 150 years.[10] In *The Compleat Angler* (first published in 1653; only the Bible and the *Book of Common Prayer* have been reprinted more often), Izaak Walton continues to recite them as articles of faith to his 'Brotherhood of the Angle'. In truth, Walton was never much of a fly-fisher. It fell to his younger friend and collaborator, Charles Cotton, to update the book in 1676 with a new section on the method.

The simple flies of the *Treatyse* look nunnish indeed compared to Cotton's elaborate creations. His patterns and their materials read like the work of some alchemist wizard: exotic

Arthur Rackman, *Izaak Walton*, 1931, etching.

Sir Peter Lely (1618–1680), *Charles Cotton*, oil on canvas.

potions of silk, feather and fur for the conjuring of trout.[11] Ingredients range from hair of bear, camel, marten, spaniel, squirrel and weasel, to whisker of cat, bristle of hog and feather of heron, ostrich and peacock. And there is more than a whiff of the witch's cauldron about his instructions. The dubbing (body material) for the Red Brown 'is to be got off the black spot of a hog's ear', and that for the Bright Brown 'is to be had out of a skinner's lime-pits, and of the hair of an abortive calf, which the lime will turn to be so bright as to shine like gold'.[12] Cotton gives this recipe for his artificial Mayfly, the Green Drake:

> The dubbing, camel's hair, bright bear's hair, the soft down that is combed from a hog's bristles and yellow camlet, well mixed together; the body long, and ribbed about with green silk, or rather yellow, waxed with green wax, the

whisks of the tail, of the long hairs of sables, or fitchet [polecat], and the wings of the white-gray feather of a mallard dyed yellow; which also is to be dyed thus. Take the root of a barbary-tree, and shave it, and put to it woody viss, with as much alum as a walnut, and boil your feathers in it with rain-water; and they will be of a very fine yellow.[13]

In Walton and Cotton we can already detect the social fault line down which Britain's angling ranks would later split. One, the self-made son of a Stafford innkeeper, was a no-nonsense bait angler, the other, a landed aristocrat who devoted his life to wine, women and country pursuits. Cotton was the archetype of the English gentlemen who could afford to indulge in what came to be styled the 'art' of fly-fishing. The catch became gradually less important than *how* it was caught. Trout and salmon flies grew ever fancier, sprouting rare and colourful materials sourced from around the globe. Chemist and inventor Sir Humphry Davy, writing in 1832, gives an Irish Mayfly pattern he calls the Green Monkey, with 'a body of yellow monkey's fur'.[14] Exotic plumage, not least from Indian jungle cock and Chinese golden pheasant, became standard regalia.[15]

From the 1850s, dry flies were developed that floated on top of the water. Though less ornate than wet flies (flies fished under the surface) they were more exacting to tie given their smaller size and the tiny differences that characterize the insects they mimicked. The little Tup's Indispensable, for example, was named for its reputed indispensability when trout were rising to a hatch of small 'pale watery' mayflies, and because the fly's original tying asked for strands of urine-stained wool from a ram's scrotum.[16] Tup's Indispensables and their ilk were made fashionable by tweed-clad Englishmen who stalked the southern chalkstreams in Queen Victoria's twilight years. These high priests of

BOWLKER'S ART OF ANGLING.

the art cast their entomologically precise imitations upstream, not down, presenting them to the trout like natural food.

Frederic Halford, who fished Hampshire's river Test, published 33 such minutely observed flies in his *Modern Development of the Dry Fly* (1910). Representing every conceivable water-bred insect, from barely visible gnats to moth-like caddis flies, the patterns went so far as to distinguish between the two winged phases (subimago and imago, or 'dun' and 'spinner') of the brief adult existence of different mayflies. Halford went further still, giving separate patterns for the male and female subimago and imago of each species. We might need a magnifying glass to tell them apart, but trout, apparently, do not. Halford's chalkstream series is the template for anglers around the world who today

British trout flies, from Richard Bowlker, *The Art of Angling* (c. 1850).

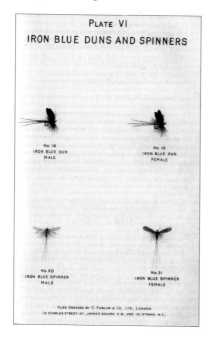

PLATE VI

IRON BLUE DUNS AND SPINNERS

No. 18
IRON BLUE DUN
MALE

No. 19
IRON BLUE DUN
FEMALE

No. 20
IRON BLUE SPINNER
MALE

No. 21
IRON BLUE SPINNER
FEMALE

FLIES DRESSED BY C. FARLOW & CO., LTD., LONDON.
(10 CHARLES STREET, ST. JAMES'S SQUARE, S.W. AND 191 STRAND, W.C.)

Halford's gender specific imitations for the two adult stages (dun and spinner) of the iron blue (*Baetis niger*), an insect about the size of a mosquito.

pit their skills against trout by 'matching the hatch'. The selectively feeding fish, rising midstream, plays up to the conceit at the heart of the sport – that trout are difficult to catch. Hence the worm fisher, with his plastic rod and bulging creel, is persona non grata.

As well as being an innovator, Halford was an influential codifier of trout fishing who sought to instil the sporting ethic of his dry fly-only philosophy. In so doing, he helped to define the 'game' and 'coarse' fishing division between gentlemen who angled for trout and salmon, and those who did not. 'By the end of the nineteenth century the method had become firmly established and the very words "fly-fishing" began to exert a strange influence,' write Buller and Falkus.[17] 'The fly-rod became the "sporting" tool of the middle and upper class angler who tended to regard anything else as being slightly suspect.' Halford compared his upstream dry-fly rule to the 'Etiquette of Golf'.[18] Taking his lead, chalkstream fisheries and fishing clubs adopted strict rules of conduct that remain in force today; club members are issued with booklets that serve as riverbank etiquette guides. However some disciples took Halford's restrictive rules of engagement too far even for him.

> They will not under any circumstances whatever make a single cast except over a rising fish, and prefer to remain idle the entire day rather than attempt to persuade the wary inhabitants of the stream to rise at an artificial fly, unless they have previously seen a natural one taken in the same position. Although respecting their scruples, this is, in my humble opinion, riding the hobby to death.[19]

Another 'high priest' who deserves mention was Halford's intellectual sparring partner G.E.M. Skues. Associated with

Hampshire's river Itchen, Skues is remembered as the inventor of nymph fishing. Critical of Halford's dry-fly orthodoxy, he applied the same imitative approach to flies for trout feeding below the surface. These he matched to the aquatic larva or 'nymphs' of river flies (a lawyer by trade, Skues saw no point waiting for hours for a hatch to occur). In the USA, there was Theodore Gordon, known as 'the father of the American school of dry-fly fishing'. A consumptive recluse who lived by the Neversink river in the Catskill Mountains in New York state, Gordon

G.E.M. Skues,
c. 1930s.

was sent a packet of dry flies by Halford in the 1890s. He took it from there, modelling his own flies on the insects eaten by American trout.[20]

In Walton's day, trout were fished with horsehair lines and very long hazel rods (up to 5.5 m/18 ft in length), often with a flexible whalebone tip.[21] We can picture Walton with Cotton at Mayfly time on their beloved river Dove, the by now venerable piscator creeping along stealthily, 'dapping' for trout.[22] This ancient method, which continues to be practiced on the limestone lakes of western Ireland, involves sticking the insects on a hook and letting the wind take the line to dance them over the surface.[23] Walton says: 'You may dape or dop . . . behind a tree, or in any deep hole; still making it to move on the top of the water, as if it were alive, and still keeping yourself out of sight, you shall certainly have sport if there be Trouts.'[24] Probably all that distinguished Cotton as the fly-fisher of the pair was the homemade Green Drake on the end of his line.

Halford and Skues witnessed the development of shorter, single-handed fly rods, designed specifically for trout (traditional

Mayflies.

A fly angler brings a trout to the net on the river Test in Hampshire, England.

double-handed rods – bulky beanpoles in comparison – were left in the hands of downstream salmon fishers). The old wood rod-building materials were replaced with the more flexible bamboo, which was less liable to break and better for fly casting. Split cane rods, constructed from triangular strips of tapered bamboo glued together, became *de rigueur*. Highly collectable today, they remain in vogue with fly-fishers who prefer the rods' handmade craftsmanship and authentic feel. Technology caught up with split cane by the 1950s, when manufacturers started switching to fibreglass. In turn, fibreglass rods were outmoded by even lighter, stronger carbon fibre models. Horsehair lines likewise evolved into silk lines, and silk into synthetic nylon.

Trout fishing had never been so popular as it was at the end of the twentieth century. In 1996 there were an estimated nine million trout anglers in America alone, according to the US Department of the Interior.[25] By 2006, the figure had fallen to seven million – a decline partly explained by demographic changes and the subsequent devastating spread of introduced whirling disease in US trout populations[26] – but trout fishers still matched the total number of teachers in the country.[27] The 2006 survey found that trout fishing remained a male-dominated sport; only one-fifth of participants were female.

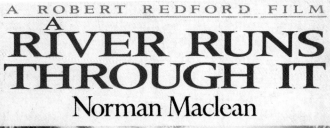

A ROBERT REDFORD FILM

A RIVER RUNS THROUGH IT

Norman Maclean

As for household income, almost a quarter of trout anglers earn $100,000 or more. Trout anglers are among the most educated anglers: 13 percent earned graduate degrees compared to 10 percent of all freshwater anglers and the US population. Trout fishing is popular among all age groups, but about half of trout anglers are 35 to 54 years old.[28]

Norman Maclean, *A River Runs Through It* (1976). This book cover features a scene from the film directed by Robert Redford in 1992.

The report also highlights the sport's importance to the rural economy: American trout anglers spent $2.5 billion on trip-related expenses (food, lodging, fishing guides and so on), $696 million on fishing tackle, $1.4 billion on purchasing fishing boats and cabins. 'The spending by trout anglers rippled through the US economy generating $13.6 billion in economic output and supported over 100 thousand jobs.'[29]

The trout-fishing spike of the 1990s has been attributed to Robert Redford's hit movie *A River Runs Through It* (1992).[30] Starring Brad Pitt and western Montana, the film, based on the autobiographical novel by Norman Maclean, chronicles the early twentieth-century coming of age of two brothers who share with their clergyman father a deep love of fly-fishing. The book begins:

> In our family, there was no clear line between religion and fly fishing. We lived at the junction of great trout rivers in western Montana, and our father was a Presbyterian minister and a fly fisherman who tied his own flies and taught others. He told us about Christ's disciples being fishermen, and we were left to assume, as my brother and I did, that all first-class fishermen on the Sea of Galilee were fly fishermen and that John, the favorite, was a dry-fly fisherman.[31]

Montana State University brands itself 'Trout U'.

President Obama tries his hand at trout fishing on the East Gallatin river, Montana, 2009.

The film's masculine period setting and Oscar-winning cinematography – Pitt's character in a felt hat casting long, beautiful arcs of sunlit line over the Blackfoot river and so on – tapped into white-collar America's nostalgic vision of an outdoors land of the free.

Not all Montanans were so happy with the outcome, however. The film is held partly responsible for an influx of wealthy hobby ranchers from Hollywood and Wall Street who bought out local farmers and priced others off their native soil. A study of the phenomenon in 2006 by researchers from the US and New Zealand warned that parts of the American West were in danger of turning into an amenity park for the rich.[32] 'The grizzled, leathery rancher riding the range to take care of his cattle and

make a buck is being replaced by wealthy "amenity" owners who fly in on weekends, fish in their private trout ponds, and often prefer roaming elk to Herefords. They don't much care whether or not the ranch turns a profit. And many of them think that wolves are neat', said the accompanying media release put out by Oregon State University.[33] 'Livestock production often takes a back seat to scenic enjoyment, fishing and solitude', the study reported. 'Money made in the booming '90s and nostalgic movies such as *A River Runs Through It* . . . helped spur a huge demand for ranches.' In the most sought-after areas of Montana and Wyoming, 60 per cent of land sold in the 1990s went to amenity buyers.

That said, Montana is proud of its trouting heritage, and benefits from the tourist revenue the sport generates. Montana State University (MSU) even brands itself 'Trout U'. Having picked up the nickname in the 1990s, owing to its historic focus on freshwater fisheries research, not to mention its enticing proximity 'to some of the country's premier trout streams' (as the university's public affairs department points out), the university trademarked 'Trout U' in 2003. Barack Obama, while campaigning in the state during his bid to become America's next president, vowed 'to get some gear and learn the art of fly fishing'.[34] In 2009 the newly elected president kept his campaign pledge when he returned to try out the pastime on the trout of the East Gallatin river. It was, said one White House correspondent, Obama's '*A River Runs Through It* moment'.[35]

Fly-fishing's aspirational appeal as a leisure activity has seen it used in advertisements for products ranging from sports utility vehicles to investment funds. The emergence of a youth subculture within the sport is attracting a younger demographic, as seen in the Angling Exploration Group's *Trout Bum Dairies*. A DVD series of high-octane adventures set to a funky soundtrack,

Known by the Company it Keeps

Volume 1: Patagonia (2005) sees these 'real life trout bums' rough-ing it across thousands of miles of South American dirt tracks for five months in pursuit of monster trout. One reviewer wrote, 'The temptation to compare the *Trout Bum Diaries* to *Endless Summer* – the '60s surf epic that marked the emergence of surf-ing as a popular lifestyle – is inescapable.'[36]

Yet it was a fly-fisherman of the old school who in the 1980s became a media phenomenon in Britain. An elderly gentleman in a tweed jacket and tie, he appeared as a character in a televi-sion commercial for the Yellow Pages telephone directory, which shows him wearily traipsing around second-hand bookshops asking for a copy of '*Fly Fishing* by J. R. Hartley'. Returning home dejected and out of luck, his daughter gives him a Yellow Pages to try. Next we see him talking on the phone. 'You do! Oh, that's wonderful!', he says, finally tracing the out-of-print volume. 'My name? Oh, yes, J. R. H-A-R-T-L-E-Y'. Affectionately parodied by comedians and on television shows, it was voted in the top fifteen of 'greatest TV ads' in a nationwide poll in 2000.[37] Such was public demand for the fictional J. R. Hartley's non-existent book that a UK publisher invented one: *Fly Fishing: Mem-ories of Angling Days* (ghosted by Michael Russell). Published in 1991, over the Christmas period alone it 'shifted an eye-watering 130,000 copies in hardback'.[38] The book's success led to two best-selling follow-ups: *J. R. Hartley Casts Again: More Memories of Angling Days* (1992) and – to accompany a new advert, in which our octogenarian hero is advised to switch to golf on health grounds – *Golfing by J. R. Hartley* (1995).

TROUT THERAPY

Perhaps he should have stuck to his original hobby: The Flyfishers' Club in Mayfair, London (a club where true-life J. R.

A trout fishing-themed Seagram's advert for whiskey, 1953.

Hartleys abound), apparently bears out the old proverb that 'time spent fishing is not deducted from your lifespan'. Some years ago the club calculated that the average age at which 62 of its most recently deceased members (all men) died was 81, exceeding by six years the national life expectancy figure for British males (then 75). Trout fishing may be life-enhancing in other ways. Casting for Recovery is a charitable group that organizes trout fishing for breast cancer sufferers for their 'mental and physical healing'. Besides the meditative aspect of fishing and its therapeutic contact with nature, the mechanics of fly casting are said to reduce tissue swelling and ease pain after a mastectomy. Founded in the US in 1996, Casting for Recovery has since spread to Britain, Ireland, Canada and New Zealand. Angling is also prescribed as an alternative 'ecotherapy' for those with depression, and has been used – with astonishing results – to tackle truancy and anti-social behaviour in young people.[39] Ted Hughes, in an interview, linked its psychological benefits to Jung's belief 'that most of his patients would be cured if only they could just re-immerse themselves in the primitive man or woman for five minutes'.[40] Fishing, the poet says, provides a 'connection with the whole living world. It gives you the opportunity of being totally immersed, turning back into yourself in a good way. A form of meditation, communion with levels of yourself that are deeper than the ordinary self.'

Meanwhile, in folk medicine, the trout has been administered as a treatment for physical ailments. A curious Turkish remedy for badly mended broken limbs involves the application of slices of mountain trout. 'Trout is cut into two pieces and applied on wrongly fixed fractured bone to loosen the bone, so that they may easily be separated and fixed correctly again.'[41]

In the late nineteenth century, the trout was prescribed as a remedy for a crisis of American virility, writes Anders Halverson.[42]

An impressive haul of trout, 1908.

The aristocratic association with game fishing in Britain reson-ated with a white ruling elite, who felt that its cosseted sons were going dangerously soft. Trout and salmon were deemed a suit-able diversion for young gentlemen that needed to 're-immerse themselves in the primitive man'. 'Such a set of black-coated, stiff-jointed, soft-muscled, paste-complexioned youth as we can boast in our Atlantic cities never before sprang from loins of Anglo-Saxon lineage,' complained physician and essayist Oliver Wendell Holmes.[43] These were concerns shared by President Theodore Roosevelt, who famously stated: 'I wish to preach, not the doctrine of ignoble ease, but the doctrine of the strenu-ous life.'[44] Urbanization was not the only concern. With black America emancipated and immigrants flocking from eastern and southern Europe, Roosevelt, using the racial language of the then fashionable eugenics movement, warned that his own kind risked committing 'race suicide'. One solution was to urge women of northern European ancestry to have more babies (foreshadowing the Aryan growth policies of Nazi Germany).

Another was to encourage the men to rediscover their vim by getting out in the woods, hunting and killing again – an excellent pastime 'for a vigorous and masterful people', Roosevelt believed.[45] Fishing, supported by a government-sponsored trout-stocking programme (see chapter Three), was promoted alongside other 'manly' recreations. In 1874 the *New York Times* stated, 'perhaps no description of outdoor sports is more generally followed or admired than that of trout fishing'.[46]

Adopting the piscine class system of the British ('coarse fish' translated to 'rough' or 'trash fish' in America), gentlemen anglers saw in trout a fishy reflection of themselves. They 'inhabit the fairest regions of nature's beautiful domain. They drink only from the purest fountains, and subsist upon the choicest food their pellucid streams supply'.[47] However, 'no fish which inhabit foul or sluggish water can be "game-fish". It is impossible from the very circumstances of their surroundings and associations'.[48]

LEWD TROUT

But before the cult of fly-fishing elevated the trout, another method of catching it resulted in coarse allusions to the fish. Thomas Cogan, in *The Haven of Health* (1584), wrote that the trout 'loueth flatterie; for being in the water it will suffer it selfe to be rubbed and clawed, and so to be taken. Whose example I wish no maydes to folow, lest they repent after clappes.' This Tudor piece of teenage sex advice refers to trout 'tickling' or 'groping', an ancient technique requiring considerable guile as the hunter uses only his bare hands. The fish tickler lies hidden on his front by a stream, in which he carefully submerges an arm. Finding an unsuspecting trout, he gently strokes its belly, lulling the fish into such a felicitous state that the hand is allowed to creep slowly to the gills; then, with a sudden grab, it is whisked onto the bank. In his *Merry Passages and Jests* (pre-1650), Sir Nicholas Le Strange says, 'A wanton wench is of the nature of a Troute, for it loves allwayes to be tickled'; and in 1654 the smutty Royalist periodical *Mercurius Fumigosus* talks of 'a two-legg'd she-Trout' caught by 'tickling her . . . into a muck sweat'.[49]

Shakespeare also recruited the trout for sexual innuendo. In *Measure for Measure*, Claudio, on his arrest for sex out of wedlock, is accused of 'groping for trouts in a peculiar river' (Act I, Scene ii). And in *Twelfth Night*, the servant Maria, while conspiring to dupe Malvolio into believing Olivia loves him, says, 'Lie thou there; for here comes the trout that must be caught with tickling' (Act II, Scene v).

Even anglers may admit to something earthily sexual in the act of catching trout. George Melly, the British jazz singer, writer and raconteur, spares no blushes in *Hooked!*, his fishing memoirs. He relates this experience while fly-fishing on the river Usk in Wales (be warned: J. R. Hartley it is not):

English trout ticklers, 1910.

I hooked and grassed a large trout. I was wading at the time down the side of a long but narrow island, impenetrable in summer because of its chest-high weeds. On impulse, the dead trout in one hand and using the closed net as a kind of machete, I carved a path through this mini-rainforest until I'd found a small clearing. There I laid the beautifully marked fish on a tree stump as if it were a sacrifice, and lying down where I could see it (a ludicrous sight, no doubt, in my thigh-high waders), masturbated into a large dock leaf.[50]

'If I could choose a death', Melly adds, 'it would be to be discovered on a river bank dead but with a smile on my face, and a big, beautifully marked trout on the grass beside me'.

TROUT FISHING IN AMERICA

Richard Brautigan attempts to commune with nature on a similar level in his loosely autobiographical novel, *Trout Fishing in America* (1967). During the narrator's incredible but thwarted

John Courage beer mat depicting a trout tickler.

search for trout fishing in America, he finds himself skinny dipping with his 'woman' in a creek where there is a hot spring full of green slime and dead trout.[51] 'I began to get ideas, as they say', which leads, ultimately, to:

> My sperm came out into the water, unaccustomed to the light, and instantly it became a misty, stringy kind of thing and swirled out like a falling star, and I saw a dead fish come forward and float into my sperm, bending it in the middle. His eyes were stiff like iron.

An encounter more soiled than erotic, and one that ends in *coitus interruptus*, it is symptomatic of the narrator's frustrated quest for an American Eden.

Brautigan's dead fish recall a passage in Ernest Hemingway's story 'Big Two-Hearted River' in which Nick Adams fishes a stretch of defiled river: 'Nick had again and again come on dead trout, furry with white fungus, drifted against a rock, or floating belly up in some pool.'[52] For Hemingway, as for Adams, the trout was a significant animal. A lifelong angler, who as a young journalist wrote fishing articles for Toronto's *Star Weekly*, Hemingway repeatedly sends his embattled male characters in search of trout as a source of spiritual and emotional succour and strength. In 'Now I Lay Me', Adams lies seriously wounded in an army tent in Italy during the First World War (as Hemingway did after being hit by mortar fire in 1918). Traumatized from shell shock and unable to sleep, Adams tries to gather his mind by fishing his favourite trout stream in his memory. He 'fishes its whole length very carefully', reconstructing soothing locations and experiences.[53] Adams's recuperation continues in 'Big Two-Hearted River', when he returns home to Michigan and goes trout

Ernest Hemingway
with two rainbow
trout in Idaho,
1939.

fishing (where the author fished in his youth). He finds the sur-
rounding landscape burnt and scarred by fire, but the trout and
the river are mostly how he remembers.

Nick looked down into the clear, brown water, colored
from the pebbly bottom, and watched the trout keeping

themselves steady in the current with wavering fins. As he watched them they changed their positions again by quick angles, only to hold steady in the fast water again. Nick watched them a long time.[54]

In so doing, he holds steady, too. As Gregory Sojka notes, trout fishing helps Adams exorcise his demons and regain his mental equilibrium.[55]

The trout is also a fixed point in an uncertain world for Robert Jordan in *For Whom the Bell Tolls*, set in the Spanish Civil War. In the climactic scene of the novel, when Jordan is fixing explosives to the underside of a bridge while under enemy fire, he composes himself by focusing on the sound of the mountain river and on the rising trout he spies far beneath him.[56]

In *The Sun Also Rises*, we have Jake Barnes, another youthful war veteran. Escaping the decadence of bohemian life in Paris, Barnes and fellow American Bill Gorton (again following in the author's footsteps) go fishing in the icy streams of the Spanish Pyrenees, where the trout 'were beautifully colored and firm and hard from the cold water'.[57] Revitalized and redeemed in body and soul, they pay a visit to the nearby Augustine monastery of Roncesvalles in the company of a fly-fishing Englishman named Harris. Bill says: 'It isn't the same as fishing, though, is it?' 'I say not', Harris agrees.[58] Sojka comments: 'Orthodox religion has given way to the sacred rite of trout fishing.'[59]

Running deep in American literature, trout have come to symbolize a natural, innocent America, and its fouling by Western consumerist society. Brautigan's *Trout Fishing in America* is a social commentary on America in the tradition of its great backwoods philosopher and soul-searcher Henry Thoreau. It reads like Thoreau's *Walden* on magic mushrooms. Brad Hayden, in an essay tying the two works, writes:

In Brautigan's novel the trout stream is a central metaphor for the shrinking American wilderness and the social values which are associated with it. The narrator of Brautigan's novel seeks a pastoral life in nature but does not succeed; his search ends in frustration and disillusionment.[60]

Beginning his quest, the trout is like some mythical creature, remembered by 'a stepfather of mine' (there were several in Brautigan's own dislocated childhood): 'The old drunk told me about trout fishing. When he could talk, he had a way of describing trout as if they were a precious and intelligent metal'.[61] When the narrator does encounter trout, they are often dead, deformed, or otherwise victims of man's unnatural acts.

In the chapter 'Trout Death by Port Wine', his fishing partner dispatches a trout by pouring port down its mouth. 'The trout went into a spasm. Its body shook very rapidly like a telescope during an earthquake. The mouth was wide open and chattering almost as if it had human teeth.'[62] 'The Cleveland Wrecking Yard', the title of another chapter, becomes the wrecking yard for a trout stream, where it is broken up and sold by the foot.

> 'You can buy as little as you want or you can buy all we've got left. A man came in here this morning and bought 563 feet. He's going to give it to his niece for a birthday present,' the salesman said. 'We're selling the waterfalls separately of course, and the trees and birds, flowers, grass and ferns we're also selling extra. The insects we're giving away free with a minimum purchase of ten feet of stream.'[63]

In Brautigan's vision of a morally bankrupt, materially driven world, even trout rivers can be packaged up and sold. Publication of this spaced-out masterpiece in 1967, six years after it was written, was perfectly timed. It captured the counterculture zeitgeist of Brautigan's small San Francisco community from which that year sprang the 'Summer of Love', a defining event of the 1960s.[64] Sales of the novel quickly hit one million copies.

Brautigan and Hemingway, later beset by drink and health issues, would both kill themselves by putting guns to their heads. In William Faulkner's *The Sound and the Fury*, Quentin Compson, contemplating suicide by drowning, watches a large old trout from a bridge, a fish that has been there for years, despite the best efforts of local anglers.

> I saw a shadow hanging like a fat arrow stemming into the current ... The arrow increased without motion, then in a quick swirl the trout lipped a fly beneath the surface with that sort of gigantic delicacy of an elephant picking up a peanut. The fading vortex drifted away down stream and then I saw the arrow again, nose into the current, wavering delicately to the motion of the water.[65]

Richard Brautigan fly-fishing for trout in Armstrong Creek, Montana, 1972.

Deciphering meaning in this Southern Gothic novel is not straightforward, to say the least. Yet the permanence of the trout's looming presence in the river Compson will shortly drown himself in appears to be symbolic of the eternity he seeks in the purging 'clean flame' of hell.

Hope in Faulkner's dark novel clings to its themes of resurrection and renewal. The same could be said of Cormac McCarthy's Pulitzer Prize-winning *The Road* (2006). This postapocalyptic tale follows the grim journey of a nameless father and son across a burnt and devastated landscape (shades of 'Big Two-Hearted River') where the sole living thing left to eat or encounter is other people. The father stares into the lifeless rivers they pass, 'where once he'd watched trout swaying in the current, tracking their perfect shadows on the stones beneath'.[66] Or where once he 'watched the flash of trout deep in a pool, invisible to see in the tea-colored water except as they turned on their sides to feed. Reflecting back the sun deep in the darkness like a flash of knives in a cave.'[67] McCarthy returns to the image of trout in the book's closing passage, when with the death of the father the son is saved (the boy has the 'breath of God', a woman says mystically):

> Once there were brook trout in the streams in the mountains. You could see them standing in the amber current where the white edges of their fins wimpled softly in the flow . . . On their backs were vermiculate patterns that were maps of the world in its becoming. Maps and mazes. Of a thing which could not be put back. Not be made right again. In the deep glens where they lived all things were older than man and they hummed of mystery.[68]

In this cryptic ending, the brook trout embodies the beauty and wonder of the natural world man has destroyed. But it is a world older and deeper than human understanding; there is the promise of resurrection and renewal in that thought. Whether we will be part of it – our hopes rest here in the son – is debatable.

6 Wild Trout

In the wild places of the Western imagination, few animals are as iconic as the trout. 'A trout', wrote Ted Hughes, 'seems "wilder" than any other fish. The falcon among fish. The wildness of empty hills, bleak and rocky lakes, frayed wilderness rivers knotting into dark pools, worst weather, desolation.'[1] The poet evokes the weather-beaten uplands of the western British Isles, its Celtic fringes; tumbling, peat-stained waters, the glimmer of red-spotted trout.

In North America, trout lead to the wild backcountry: pine-scented mountains, pristine lakes, the virgin frontiers of Lewis and Clark. The promise of trout is the promise that such places still exist. Hiking in the Blue Ridge Mountains of the eastern US, nature writer Christopher Camuto seeks out the final 'vestiges of wildness':

> A few stands of virgin timber, some uninterrupted vistas, a remnant black bear population, some bobcat and timber rattlers, a few undisturbed habitats where flora and fauna persist, and the most subtle form that wildness takes – the quicksilver presence of wild trout.[2]

In delineating the mountains' wild vestiges, the brook trout is his reference. Recalling the imagery of the concluding passage of

John Singer Sargent, *Trout Stream in the Tyrol*, 1914, oil on canvas.

Cormac McCarthy's *The Road*, Camuto writes: 'The convoluted ribbing of contour lines on the topographical maps reminds me of the vermiculation on a brook trout's back and makes some important connections between trout and land clear.' Ted Leeson, another US writer who maps the natural environment by its trout, says, 'What is as important as the trout is that trout-shaped space that we carve around it.'[3]

The trout surfaces in other art forms as an expression of wild places and the sense of wonder in nature. Musically, it is best known as the inspiration for Franz Schubert's 'Trout' quintet, a piece that transports the listener to the mountains and forests of the Austrian Alps, where the Viennese composer loved to go walking. Partly based on his earlier song *Die Forelle* ('The Trout'), a popular ditty about an angler seducing a coy trout in an alpine brook, Schubert delightfully interplays the movement of the fish with the liquid flow of the stream as it darts in

Quintet in A Major, Op. 114 ("Trout")

and out of view, lifting to the surface, then merging again with the current.

In art, besides being a favourite subject of sporting artists, the trout has caught the eye of such painters as Winslow Homer. One of America's foremost nineteenth-century artists, Homer's portfolio suggests that he was fairly smitten with the brook trout – not surprisingly, given the fish's hot colours and dazzling constellation of spots (think of a starlit sky over a melting sunset glow). An avid fly fisher, Homer went trouting in New York State, Maine and beyond. 'Like other urban refugees who ventured into the wilderness for rejuvenation, Homer came to rely upon these backwoods forays', writes Robert M. Poole.[4] 'The excursions also provided another market for his watercolors,

Winslow Homer, *Leaping Trout*, 1886, watercolour over graphite pencil.

Winslow Homer, *Trout Fishing, Lake St John, Quebec*, 1895, watercolour.

which were snapped up by anglers, hunters and a growing community of outdoor enthusiasts.' Poole says Homer's fishing scenes 'were noted for their fluidity, their understated grace and their feeling for the empty spaces'.

Nowhere were the trout spaces wilder or emptier than in the American West. There, nineteenth-century explorers reported an extraordinary abundance of trout. The white man, hardly believing his luck, launched into them with the same gusto as he did the unfortunate American buffalo. In 1834 John Townsend, camped by the Green river in Wyoming, wrote in his journal: 'Old Isaac [sic] Walton would be in his glory here, and the precautionary measures which he so strongly recommends in approaching a trout stream, he would not need to practice, as the fish is not shy, and bites quickly and eagerly at a grasshopper or minnow.'[5] In 1882 Edward R. Hewitt, fishing for camp food one day on the edge of Yellowstone Park, landed so many trout that by mid-afternoon he had filled enough sacks for three pack mules.[6] 'I was not sorry to quit as I was really tired out', Hewitt confessed. He put the total weight of the fish, minus their innards, at between 205 and 225 kg (450 and 500 lb).

People have even wondered if, in 1876, this incredible bounty of trout had a hand in General Custer's last stand in the Battle of the Little Bighorn.[7] Custer commanded one of three US Cavalry detachments engaged in rounding up Native American coalition forces led by Sitting Bull. However the detachment under General George Crook was waylaid by battle and, from the sound

F. Palmer, *The Trout Stream*, 1852, lithograph.

of it, by excellent fishing in and around Wyoming's Tongue river. Captain John Bourke, a staff officer with Crook, recorded:

> The credulity of the reader will be taxed to the utmost limit if he follow my record of the catches of trout made in all these streams . . . but the hundreds and thousands of fine fish taken from that set of creeks by officers and soldiers, who had nothing but the rudest of appliances, speaks to the wonderful resources of the country.[8]

General Crook, who had not forgotten to bring his angling gear with him, rather than pressing on with the advance as planned, waited for supplies and reinforcements at his riverside camp: 'For two weeks Crook tarried, hunting and fishing all the while.'[9] Custer and his men were slaughtered in the meantime.

The Apache, writes Bourke, 'could not be persuaded to touch anything with scales upon it', which might partly explain the multitude of trout.[10] The Shoshones, who sided with US forces during this campaign, 'had more sense'. Bourke says their fishing method involved making a dam of 'rocks and wattle-work of willow' into which the fish were corralled and trapped. Mounted on ponies, they drove the trout towards the dam, 'lashing the surface of the stream in their front with long poles, and all the while joining in a wild medicine song'. By Bourke's reckoning, Crook's men polished off at least 15,000 fish in three weeks. 'The whole command was living upon trout or as much as it wanted.' The US Army provisioning itself by going around devouring the trout seems an apt metaphor for the subjugation of the Wild West. Bourke provides another when he and some soldiers, taking a bath, plunge naked into a river, 'greatly to the astonishment of a school of trout of all sizes which circled about and darted in and out among the rocks, trying to determine who and what we were . . . the first white men to penetrate to that seclusion'.[11] The anthropomorphizing speaks for itself.

The English trout traditionally inhabits an altogether gentler, more intimate landscape, of soft, human contours. It is the pastoral countryside of Walton's *Compleat Angler*, where 'the earth feeds man, and all those several beasts that both feed him, and afford him recreation'.[12] And where, after a day's pleasant recreation, Walton's protagonists retire to the local inn: 'And now let's move toward our lodging, and drink a draught of Red-cow's milk as we go, and give pretty Maudlin and her honest mother a brace of trouts for their supper.'[13] The rustic sign of the trout still hangs outside many English pubs, such as the The Lazy Trout, Rising Trout, Speckled Trout, Tickled Trout, Trout and Tipple, or, more commonly, plain old Trout.[14]

The Trout Inn,
Itchen Abbas,
Hampshire,
England.

Westward-Ho!, Charles Kingsley's Elizabethan high seas adventure, sets off from for the 'boundless Western Ocean' from the secluded combes of north Devon, each with a 'crystal trout stream winding across and across from one hill-foot to the other', and 'where the salmon-trout [sea trout] gather in from their Atlantic wanderings'.[15] Richard Jefferies, the Victorian nature writer, locates the trout even closer to home in *Nature Near London* (1883), his study of the secret wildlife of the suburbs.[16] He tells the story of 'a London trout' that lived in a brook in the shadow of a bridge, where the writer observed it discreetly for three consecutive summers. 'It is wonderful to think how difficult it is to see anything under one's very eyes, and thousands of people walked actually and physically right over the fish.' In the fourth year, Jefferies shared his secret. 'I took friends to look at this wonderful fish, which defied all the loafers and poachers' and which 'threw a mental shadow over the minds of passers-by, so that they never thought of the possibility of such

A specimen trout caught in the river Colne near London, 1901.

146

a thing as trout'. But soon afterwards the brook was dammed above the bridge, 'that some accused main or pipe or other horror might be laid'. Jefferies spotted the trout trapped in a muddy pool under a tree, the water too shallow to cover its back. 'He was swimming round to try and find out the reason of this sudden stinting of room.' Jefferies did not see the fish again. 'I never failed to glance over the parapet into the shadowy water. Somehow it seemed to look colder, less pleasant that it used to do. The spot was empty, and the shrill winds whistled through the poplars.' Jefferies's lament for the lost trout was to become a familiar one.

POLLUTED WATERS

Over the next century, population growth and industrialization accelerated the trout's 'stinting of room'. Pollution from burning fossil fuels descended from the sky as acid rain, often many hundreds of miles from its source. Much of the fallout from acid rain-making gases (sulphur dioxide and nitrogen oxides) that were spewed from cities in Britain landed on forests and lakes in Scandinavia (earning the UK the moniker 'Dirty Man of Europe'). Norwegians held up the trout as evidence of the environmental damage this was causing. Research in southern Norway indicated that by 1983 the effects of water acidification had wiped out brown trout in 1,631 lakes, with some regions losing close to 70 per cent of their populations.[17]

International agreements followed that forced governments and industry to act, and cleaner emissions technology removed acid rain from the headlines. Today perhaps the major pollution threat to stillwater trout habitats is eutrophication. A consequence of nitrates, phosphates and other nutrients leaching into waters, the main sources are fertilizers washed off fields and

The Ohrid trout, depicted on an Albanian stamp.

effluents from wastewater treatment works. The nutrients promote algal blooms that starve the water of oxygen when the algae decomposes, suffocating life.

Lake Ohrid, shared by Albania and Macedonia, is said to be the oldest lake in Europe. Formed about three million years ago, this watery 'museum of living fossils' provided sanctuary to prehistoric species killed off elsewhere by a succession of ice ages.[18] The UNESCO World Heritage Site supports in excess of 200 endemic species, ten of them fish, including its very own trout, *Salmo letnica*. A prized local delicacy, the Ohrid trout is the lake's defining species. Indeed, when the famous tenor José Carreras was announced as being booked to open the Ohrid Summer Festival in 2005, organizers said they would serve the fish in his honour, apparently forgetting the fishing ban on the trout then in force.[19] The (widely flouted) ban was in response to dwindling stocks of the commercially important species; added to the World Conservation Union's Red List of endangered species in 1996, the trout has latterly become the emblem of a looming ecological disaster. On top of overfishing, eutrophication caused by flows of untreated sewage and urban development around the lake threaten to tip it from being oligotrophic (gin clear and low in nutrients – the condition of pristine trout lakes) to eutrophic (cloudy and high in nutrients), leading to summer stagnation and dangerously low oxygen levels. In 2003 the lake's phosphorous load was estimated to be three to five times greater than it ought to be to keep it in an oligotrophic state.[20] If environmental protection measures fail to reverse the decline, Ohrid's 'living fossil' trout could be wiped out, along with other unique ice age relics.

In Britain, the pellucid trout streams of Walton's fishing landscape have likewise been sullied by eutrophication, causing outbreaks of algae that smother gravels and coat aquatic plants in

148

a slimy brown film. The renowned chalk-fed trout rivers have also had to cope with being drained of their life force to meet the competing demands of spreading suburbia, with its power showers, washing machines and swimming pools. Increased groundwater extraction from chalk aquifers since the 1960s led to drastically reduced flows. There are years when some daintier chalkstreams vanish altogether, as highlighted by WWF. (It is a measure of the importance of these rivers to England's natural heritage that the global conservation organization has taken up their cause.[21])

There is no respite for wild trout in the ocean, either. Sea trout stocks have been decimated by infestations of parasites that abound in coastal waters where salmon farming occurs. Sea lice – small crustaceans that attach to fish to feed on their mucus, skin and blood – are natural parasites of salmon and trout in saltwater. However, around salmon farms, where open water cages holding hundreds of thousands of fish act as super breeding grounds, sea lice concentrations rocket. Until the 1980s, Loch Maree in the West Highlands of Scotland had a reputation as one of the world's premier fishing destinations for sea trout; then, in the space of a few years, the run dwindled almost to nothing. In 1985, the year salmon farming began near the mouth of the river Ewe (the loch's link to the sea), the average catch by guests at the Loch Maree Hotel was almost 1,100 fish.[22] By 1989 the figure had fallen by 90 per cent. In 2000 barely 50 sea trout were caught. Alan Jackson, a fishing guide who then worked for the hotel, said, 'Catches of ten fish per boat, each weighing between six to ten pounds (2.7 to 4.5 kilograms), used to be common. Now you consider yourself lucky to land a single sea trout, never mind its size.'[23] But the rare fish that came to the net was not always a welcome sight. 'There's one in particular that's etched on my mind', he said. 'But for its eyeballs it was completely pink, a festering sore with only the stubs of its fins remaining. It was being eaten alive by hundreds of immature sea lice.'

For the Scottish government to permit this onslaught to continue so long – despite the weight of scientific evidence – shows where its priorities lie.[24] Industrial salmonid trumps wild salmonid. Yet this is quite needless, according to groups that campaign to protect the marine environment from the impacts of open water salmon farming, impacts that go way beyond sea trout. Closed-system installations on land or water 'would minimise escapes, prevent the transfer of parasites and the spread of disease, and allow waste effluents to be collected and treated in order to avoid pollution', the UK's Salmon & Trout Association reiterated in 2010.[25] The association's Paul Knight concluded, 'It must be the Government's statutory responsibility, and the industry's moral one, to protect two of Scotland's most valuable and iconic natural resources – wild salmon and sea trout – before it is too late.'

A Scottish sea trout suffering from an infestation of sea lice.

With the spectre of global warming, the coldwater-loving trout again finds itself on the environmental frontline. The US Forest Service, for instance, flags up the likely impact of forecast warming of mountain streams with predictions that the southern Appalachian range will become too hot to handle for more than 50 per cent of its wild trout, and that up to 90 per cent of the US's endangered bull trout will disappear.[26] Other research, led by the Natural Resources Defense Council (NRDC), warns that a nearly 2.7°C (5°F) temperature rise by the end of this century would see trout habitat shrink by more than half in the Rocky Mountain region.[27] 'Trout are one of the best indicators of healthy river ecosystems; they're the aquatic version of the canary in the coalmine', NRDC's Theo Spencer said in 2008. 'This is our wake up call that urgent action is needed today to reduce heat-trapping pollution that causes global warming.'

RETURNING TROUT

The prominence of trout as ecological indicator species is in no small part down to conservation-minded members of their angling fan base. Trout Unlimited, founded in 1959, has as its raison d'être 'conserving, protecting and restoring North America's coldwater fisheries and their watersheds'. It has grown into an effective lobbyist for wild trout, boasting (in 2011) in excess of 135,000 members and a staff of some 120 scientists, lawyers and administrators. Adopting American angler Lee Wulff's maxim, 'a good game fish is too valuable to be caught only once', Trout Unlimited was from its inception a champion of catch-and-release and the use of barbless hooks. The practice might seem a perversion of the natural instinct to hunt in order to eat, but, despite some stiff opposition, the conservation argument is winning out. Catch-and-release has become standard on trout waters where native stocks would not otherwise withstand the level of fishing pressure. As a consequence, wild trout are reclaiming waters from their farmed replacements. 'We're seeing more thought to managing for native and wild fish these days, and more reliance on habitat rather than hatcheries', comments Robert Behnke.[28] In Britain and Ireland, the Wild Trout Trust, a charity set up in 1997, carries out river surveys that result in the addition of almost 100 miles (150 km) of upgraded trout habitat every year.[29]

The story comes full circle with the story of a London trout river. The Wandle makes its half-buried passage through the concrete sprawl of south London, emerging from a cryptic riverscape of kebab shops, office blocks and A-roads to meet the Thames at the heart of Western Europe's largest city. It once ranked among England's finest trout streams. Two centuries ago, the loss of an arm and the sight in one eye did not prevent Lord Nelson fishing the Wandle. 'Nelson was a good fly-fisher, and as proof of his passion for it, continued the pursuit even with his left hand', recalled Sir Humphry Davy.[30] Nelson, who shared a house on the river with his mistress, Lady Hamilton, called the place 'Paradise Merton', and Davy talked about fishing 'in the shady green meadows by the bright clear streams of the Wandle'.[31] But the swift, constant flows of this chalkstream, which rises on the North Downs, had other uses. Harnessed to power watermills, at one stage an 11-mile (18-km) section supported some 90 mills, producing everything from silk and snuff to copper and gunpowder. Gradually, as the city expanded and industrial processes developed, pollution began to overwhelm the little river. John Ruskin, the eminent Victorian art critic, was not insensitive to its plight:

No clearer or diviner waters ever sang with the constant lips of the hand which 'giveth rain from heaven'; no pastures

ever lightened in the spring-time with more passionate
blossoming . . . but, with deliberate mind I say, that I
have never seen anything so ghastly in its inner tragic
meaning – not in Pisan Maremma – not by Campagna
tomb – not by the sand-isles of the Torcellan shore – as
the slow stealing of aspects of reckless, indolent, animal
neglect, over the delicate sweetness of that English scene:
nor is any blasphemy or impiety – any frantic saying or
godless thought – more appalling to me, using the best
power of judgment I have to discern its sense and scope,
than the insolent defilings of those springs by the human
herds that drink of them.[32]

By the early twentieth century the river was in its death
throes. 'In the late 1960s, the Wandle was officially designated
an open sewer', said local resident and Wandle activist Alan

A wild brown trout
from South Uist,
Outer Hebrides,
Scotland.

153

Suttee.[33] 'And in the '70s I remember it running red, pink or blue, depending on what dye they were using in the local tanneries.' In 2002 the Wandle presented another striking image: a fisherman wading on bright gravels by Merton High Street, casting a dry fly between waving tresses of aquatic greenery. 'If you pull out a handful of weed, it's crawling with shrimps and other bugs', Suttee said. 'We've been seeing huge barbel, chub, perch and rudd.'

This riverine Lazarus act is attributed to the collapse of heavy industry in the 1980s, and a nationwide drive to tackle urban river pollution through improved wastewater treatment technology.[34] The Wandle is becoming a trout stream again, and local schoolchildren are being recruited to restore its iconic fish. 'Trout in the Classroom', a concept developed in North America, is an environmental education programme that encourages children to engage in the natural world around them. London schools in the Wandle catchment area are supplied with specially adapted tanks so some 9,000 children each year can raise baby brown trout from eggs. These classroom trout are then released into the river, hopefully to kickstart natural regeneration. The scheme is supported by the Wandle Trust, an environmental charity dedicated to restoring and maintaining the health of the river. Its teams of volunteers regularly meet to remove 'the insolent defilings' of today's human herds. A typical haul – made during a clean-up in August 2010 – included 25 tyres, a sports car, three scooters, four computers, a wheelchair, a washing machine and a life-size model of Superwoman. But the real find was made earlier that year: a tiny trout fry – the first wild-born Wandle trout recorded in at least 80 years.[35] Detected during an invertebrate survey, news of the fish was announced by one of its discoverers, Theo Pike, on the Wandle Trust website. His headline: 'A trout to echo round the world . . .'.

Let us hope it marks a bright new chapter for the London trout, and in our evolving relationship with this wonderful creature. We have seen the trout revered, lauded, propagated, exported, scientifically altered, devoured, trashed and, finally, revived. Our intertwined histories have made the fish a totem of our Jekyll-and-Hyde response to nature. We celebrate the trout for its vitality and wildness, yet domicile it and mass-produce it in concrete tanks; we have gone to amazing lengths to establish the fish in the farthest reaches of the world, yet pollute and degrade its waters at our own back doors; we seek to preserve genetically distinct strains, yet alter the fish with DNA from other animals. We cannot help but be struck by the irony of these contradictions, and ask ourselves how, given our esteem for the trout, we could have treated it so.

People once sought audiences with sacred trout to know their futures. Perhaps we seek the fish for the same reason today. We who glance over the parapet of our hurly-burly existence look into the shadowy water for reassurance. For the reassurance of this wild, beautiful presence. For the possibility of such a glorious thing as trout.

Timeline of the Trout

c. 50 million BC	c. 12 million BC	21,000 BC	AD 54–68
The first known salmonid ancestor of trout, *Eosalmo driftwoodensis*, appears in the fossil record in Eocene lake sediments in British Columbia, Canada	The sabre-tooth salmon (*Oncorhynchus rastrosus*), a giant fossil relative of the rainbow trout, swims in prehistoric seas	Clear evidence for the consumption of trout (*Salmo trutta*) is left by humans living in caves in northwest Spain. Even older, unidentified salmonid remains indicate trout may have been on the menu more than 35,000 years ago.	Emperor Nero orders the construction of the tallest dams known in the Roman world in the Apennine mountains to create pleasure lakes where he can go trout fishing

1653	1758	1805	1852	1864
Izaak Walton's *The Compleat Angler* is published. A section on fly-fishing and trout flies by Walton's friend, Charles Cotton, is added in 1676.	Carl Linnaeus pins the European brown trout with a scientific label, *Salmo trutta*	The historic Lewis and Clark Expedition to the American West introduces white Americans to the cutthroat trout (*Oncorhynchus clarkii*)	The trout breeding methods of two French peasants lead to the establishment of the world's first industrial fish farm at Huningue in France	The trout is launched on the wider world with a three-month voyage from England to Tasmania

1950s	1959	1967	1980s	1992
Millions of fingerling trout are rained down on US mountain lakes from aircraft during a massive aerial stocking programme	Trout Unlimited, a conservation group dedicated to protecting and restoring trout and salmon and their coldwater habitats, is founded in the US	Richard Brautigan's cult novel *Trout Fishing in America* is published	Salmon farming becomes established in coastal waters around northwest Scotland, with devastating consequences for sea trout populations	The hit movie *A River Runs Through It* is released, helping to push the number of trout anglers in the US to nine million

c. 200	1420	1496	1541

Roman author Aelian writes about the fishing of trout in Macedonia using artificial flies made of wool and feather

French monk Dom Pinchon is said to have penned a now elusive manuscript which describes how to propagate trout artificially

A Treatyse of Fysshynge Wyth an Angle is published. Packed with trout fishing tips, it is the earliest text on angling in printed English.

Spanish conquistadors on a quest to find the fabled Seven Cities of Gold provide the earliest account of American trout

1876	1883	1920S	1928

Soldiers serving under General Crook during the US Army's western campaign against Native American forces catch and eat an estimated 15,000 trout in just three weeks

The brown trout makes landfall in North America as a consignment of eggs shipped to New York from Germany

Austrian inventor Viktor Schauberger's quest to harness Earth's natural energies for new technologies is inspired by his observations of trout and their streams while working as a forest warden

A giant trout weighing 31 kg (68 lb) is caught in Lake Maggiore, Switzerland

2000	2001	2007	2010	2010

The brown and rainbow trout make the top '100 of the World's Worst Invasive Alien Species', a list compiled by the World Conservation Union

The sex lives of trout are splashed in the papers when researchers report that female brown trout fake their orgasms as a breeding strategy

Scientists in Japan announce they have successfully bred trout using lab-altered salmon as parents

A transgenic trout created using cattle-type DNA is revealed, which grows 15 to 20 per cent more meat than normal trout

Wild-born trout are detected in London's river Wandle after an absence of more than 80 years

References

INTRODUCTION

1 John Gierach, with a foreword by Gary LaFontaine, *Trout Bum* (London, 1993), n.p. LaFontaine also writes, 'Trout bums are as intelligent, perceptive, talented, and well educated as other fly fishermen. Maybe they make less money per year than most fly fishermen, but that has to be by choice. If "bums" is a negative term it is precisely because such people are poverty stricken not by circumstance but by self-determination.'

2 Gierach, *Trout Bum*, p. 7.

3 John Batchelor, *The Ainu and their Folk-lore* (London, 1901), pp. 51–5.

4 Paul Schullery, 'Imperialist Trout', first published in *American Angler* magazine (2005): www.midcurrent.com/articles/history/schullery_imperialist _trout.aspx (accessed 6 May 2011).

5 Izaak Walton and Charles Cotton, *The Compleat Angler* [1676] (London, 1844), p. 66.

6 L. Patrick Coyle, *The World Encyclopedia of Food* (New York, 1982), p. 689.

7 Darin Kinsey, '"Seeding the Water as the Earth": The Epicenter and Peripheries of a Western Aquacultural Revolution', *Environmental History*, XI/3 (2006), pp. 527–66.

8 Anders Halverson, *An Entirely Synthetic Fish: How Rainbow Trout Beguiled America and Overran the World* (New Haven, CT, 2010), p. 73.

9 *Science*, CCCXVII/5844 (September 2007), p. 1517.

10 James Owen, 'Would You Adam and Eve it?', *Trout and Salmon* (September 2009), pp. 24–5.
11 Callum Coats, *Living Energies: Viktor Schauberger's Brilliant Work with Natural Energy Explained* (Dublin, 2001), pp. 284–8.
12 Thomas McGuane, *The Longest Silence* (London, 2000), p. 233.
13 Ibid., p. 110.

1 VARIOUS TROUT

1 C. J. Holmes, *The Tarn and the Lake: Thoughts on Life in the Italian Renaissance* (London, 1913), p. viii.
2 Carl von Linné, *Systema Naturae* (Stockholm, 1758).
3 Robert J. Behnke, *About Trout* (Guilford, CT, 2007), p. 45.
4 Ibid.
5 Holmes, *The Tarn and the Lake*, p. viii.
6 Malcolm Greenhalgh, 'Wild Trout in the British Isles – Their Variety and Conservation', *British Wildlife* (December 2000), p. 114.
7 A. Laurence Wells, *The Observer's Book of Freshwater Fishes of the British Isles* (London, 1941), p. 52.
8 Behnke, *About Trout*, p. 45. While species designation is important in terms of conservation – since to give a threatened animal a name might mean that the authorities will do something about it – what really is important, says Behnke, is recognizing and preserving diversity *within* a species. Darwin himself recognized within-species variation as a driver of evolution.
9 Humphry Davy, *Salmonia; or, Days of Fly Fishing* [1828] (London, 1851), pp. 54–5.
10 A. Ferguson, 'The Importance of Identifying Conservation Units: Brown Trout and Pollan Biodiversity in Ireland', *Biology and Environment: Proceedings of the Royal Irish Academy* (2004), CIV/3, pp. 33–41.
11 Daniel Pauly, *Darwin's Fishes: An Encyclopedia of Ichthyology, Ecology, and Evolution* (Cambridge, 2004), p. xvii.
12 Peter Coates, *Salmon* (London, 2006), p. 15.

13 Until 1988 Pacific trout were classified in the same genus as Atlantic salmon and trout, *Salmo*. The decision to instead place rainbow and cutthroat trout in the genus *Oncorhynchus* was based on evidence of closer ties to Pacific salmon.

14 Patrick Trotter, *Cutthroat: Native Trout of the West* (Berkeley, CA, 2008), pp. 5–6.

15 Ibid., pp. 2–3. Trotter says the trout stream encountered by conquistador Coronado's expedition was located near the Pueblo city of Cicuye in the valley of the Pecos River. Coronado's hopes of finding unimaginable riches were crushed when his destination, Cibola, turned out not to be the 'Seven Cities of Gold' but a collection of poor Pueblo Indian villages.

16 Ibid.

17 C. Groot and L. Margolis, eds, *Pacific Salmon Life Histories* (Vancouver, BC, 1991), p. 449.

18 Bo Delling and Ignacio Doadrio, 'Systematics of the Trout Endemic to Moroccan Lakes, with Description of a New Species', *Ichthyological Exploration of Freshwaters*, XVI/1 (March 2005), pp. 49–64.

19 Stefan Lovgren, 'World's Largest Trout Thrives in Mongolia – For Now', *National Geographic News* (14 November 2007): http://news.nationalgeographic.com/news/2007/11/071114-taimen-mongolia.html, accessed 19 May 2011.

20 Other *Hucho* species include the endangered huchen (*H. hucho*), native to Europe's Danube basin.

21 Izaak Walton and Charles Cotton, *The Compleat Angler* [1676] (London, 1844), pp. 68–70.

22 Ibid., pp. 70–71.

23 W. E. Frost and M. E. Brown, *The Trout* (London, 1970), p. 53.

24 Personal communication.

25 Jon Copley, 'Fussy Fish Fake It', *New Scientist*, 2282 (March 2001).

26 Frost and Brown, *The Trout*, p. 80.

27 Walton, *The Compleat Angler*, p. 70.

28 Frost and Brown, *The Trout*, appendix III.

29 World record freshwater fish database edited by Heinz Machacek:

www.fishing-worldrecords.com/index.htm (accessed 6 May 2011).

30 Beatrix Potter, *The Tale of Mr Jeremy Fisher* (New York, 1906).

31 Mike Taft, letter to *The Daily Telegraph* (11 February 2005).

32 Charles Kingsley, *The Water-Babies: A Fairy Tale for a Land-baby* [1863] (London, 1907), p. 111.

33 Frost and Brown, *The Trout*, pp. 37–8.

34 James Owen, 'Silly Old Trout?', *Country Life* (31 August 1995), p. 65.

35 Behnke, *About Trout*, p. 47.

36 K. E. Overturf, et al., 'Status and Opportunities for Genomics Research with Rainbow Trout', *Comparative Biochemistry and Physiology Part B: Biochemistry and Molecular Biology*, cxxxiii/4 (December 2002), pp. 609–46.

37 'Improved Method Developed to Test Carcinogen Risk', media release, Oregon State University, June 2009: http://oregonstate.edu/ua/ncs/archives/2009/jun/improved-method-developed-test-carcinogen-risk (accessed 19 May 2011).

38 Tomoyuki Okutsu, et al.,'Production of Trout Offspring from Triploid Salmon Parents', *Science*, cccxvii/5844 (September 2007), p. 1517.

39 Olivia Judson, 'Spawning Something Fishy', *New York Times* (1 January 2008).

40 John Gierach, *Trout Bum* (London, 1993), p. 6.

41 'Fishes' Secret Sought to Add Speed to Boats', *Popular Mechanics Magazine*, xlvii/6 (June 1927), p. 900.

42 The Schauberger Archives, Linz (January 1952).

43 Callum Coats, *Living Energies: Viktor Schauberger's Brilliant Work with Natural Energy Explained* (Dublin, 2001), pp. 143–4.

44 Olof Alexandersson, *Living Water: Viktor Schauberger and the Secrets of Natural Energy* (Bath, 1990), p. 85.

45 Ibid., p. 86.

46 Ibid., pp. 88–9.

47 Ibid., p. 93. Schauberger is quoted as saying he was given the option of either complying with Himmler's demand or being hanged.

48 Victor Schauberger, 'Nature Was My Teacher', trans. Albert Zock, in *Implosion: Viktor Schauberger and the Path of Natural Energy*,

ed. Riley Hansard Crabb and Thomas Maxwell Thompson (Eureka, CA, 1985), p. 67.
49 Coats, *Living Energies*, pp. 284–6.
50 Albert Zock, 'Viktor Schauberger's Biological Submarine', *Journal of Borderland Research* (September–October 1990).
51 Michael Kanellos, 'Water Companies Taking Cue from Nature', *Greentech Media* (9 October 2008): www.greentechmedia.com/articles/read/water-companies-taking-cue-from-nature-1388 (accessed 6 May 2011).

2 SACRED TROUT

1 Gema E. Adán, et al., 'Fish as Diet Resource in North Spain During the Upper Paleolithic', *Journal of Archaeological Science*, XXXVI/3 (March 2009), pp. 895–9. According to this study, identified brown trout bones in human caves in northern Spain have been dated to around 21,000 years ago, while undetermined salmonid remains (they could also belong to salmon) date as far back as 37,000 years ago.
2 Michael P. Richards and Erik Trinkaus, 'Isotopic Evidence for the Diets of European Neanderthals and Early Modern Humans', *Proceedings of the National Academy of Sciences of the United States of America*, CVI/38 (September 2009), pp. 16034–9.
3 Ibid.
4 Peter Coates, *Salmon* (London, 2006), p. 156.
5 Paul G. Bahn, *Cave Art* (London, 2007), p. 166.
6 Janet and Colin Bord, *Sacred Water: Holy Wells and Water Lore in Britain and Ireland* (London, 1985), p. 119.
7 When the missionary monk St Augustine was sent by Rome to Britain in AD 595, it is recorded that he was given express instructions to consecrate sites of pagan worship rather than destroy them, and not to interfere with established customs.
8 Sabine Baring-Gould and John Fisher, *Lives of the British Saints*, vol. IV (London, 1913), pp. 92–3.
9 Gabriel Alington, *Borderlands: The History and Romance of the*

Herefordshire Marches (Leominster, 1998), pp. 38–9.

10 David Profumo, *In Praise of Trout* (London, 1989), p. xii.

11 Martin Martin, *A Description of the Western Islands of Scotland* (London, 1703), pp. 140–41. Martin's account of his travels was an inspiration for Samuel Johnson's famous tour of the Western Isles with James Boswell in 1773. Johnson's account, published in 1775, fails to say much about trout, however.

12 Ibid., p. 121.

13 Bord, *Sacred Water*, p. 121.

14 W. G. Wood-Martin, *Traces of the Elder Faiths in Ireland; A Folklore Sketch; A Handbook of Irish Pre-Christian Traditions*, vol. II (London, 1901), pp. 108–12.

15 Ibid., p. 112.

16 Ibid.

17 Ibid., pp. 110–11.

18 Samuel Lover, *Legends and Stories of Ireland* (London, 1853) pp. 32–44.

19 W. B. Yeats, *The Wind Among the Reeds* (London, 1899).

20 A. Norman Jeffares, *A New Commentary on the Poems of W. B. Yeats* (Stanford, CA, 1984), p. 52.

21 Profumo, *In Praise of Trout*, p. xii.

22 Bord, *Sacred Water*, p. 4.

23 Excavations around Stonehenge were carried out as part of the Stonehenge Riverside Project, led by the University of Sheffield's Mike Parker-Pearson. Parker-Pearson argues that the wider Stonehenge landscape represented the realms of the living and the dead, and that the river Avon connected them. 'We think the river is acting like a conduit to the underworld', Parker-Pearson said in a 2007 interview, 'Stonehenge Settlement Found: Builders' Homes, "Cult Houses" http://news.nationalgeographic.com/news/2007/01/070130-stonehenge_2.html (accessed 20 May 2011).

24 The Ainu, the original inhabitants of Japan, are also indigenous to easternmost Russia. Following centuries of integration with ethnic Japanese, who colonized from the south, few if any pureblood Ainu remain in Japan.

25 John Batchelor, *The Ainu and their Folk-lore* (London, 1901), pp. 51–5.

26 Ibid., p. 55.

27 Ibid., p. 403.

28 Peter Rand, 'Ancient, Giant Salmon in Asia Edging Towards Extinction', Wild Salmon Center media release (23 May 2006). The release announced that the World Conservation Union (IUCN) had listed the Sakhalin taimen as 'critically endangered'.

29 James Owen, 'Can Angling Save World's Largest Salmon?', *National Geographic News* (August 2004): http://news.national-geographic.com/news/2004/08/0819_040819_taimen_fishing.html (accessed 19 May 2011).

30 Personal communication.

31 Peter Wonacott, 'Mongolia's Monks Take up New Cause: Saving Giant Salmon', *Wall Street Journal* (8 October 2004).

32 Gísli Pálsson, *Signifying Animals: Human Meaning in the Natural World*, ed. R. G. Willis (London, 1990), pp. 116–20.

33 Ibid.

34 'Furry Fin Flappers and Pelted Piscatorial Prizes', *Pueblo Chieftain* (15 November 1938): http://www.furbearingtrout.com/cheiftan.html (accessed 21 September 2011).

35 'Myth or Marvel? The Fur-bearing Trout': www.furbearingtrout.com/montanawildlife.html (accessed 19 May 2011).

3 IMPERIAL TROUT

1 Jean Walker, *Origins of the Tasmanian Trout* (Hobart, Australia, 1998). Where no other reference is given relating to the transport of the first brown trout from England to Tasmania, this work is the source.

2 'Sir James Arndell Youl (1811–1904)', online edition of the *Australian Dictionary of Biography*: www.adb.online.anu.edu.au/biogs/A060481b.htm (accessed 19 May 2011).

3 Youl said the idea of transporting fish ova packed in boxes of moss was first suggested to him in Paris. The practice does appear to have been a French innovation. Francis Francis, in his book *Fish-Culture: A Practical Guide to the Modern System of Breeding and Rearing Fish* (London and New York, 1865), notes that early consignments of fish eggs sent from northern France were packed in layers of damp moss.

4 Arthur Nicols, *The Acclimatisation of the Salmonidae at the Antipodes* (London, 1882), p. 20.

5 In a letter to *The Field* in September 1879, Francis Francis said he obtained his brown trout ova from the Wey at Alton, Hampshire, and from the Wye at High Wycombe, Buckinghamshire.

6 Salmon Ponds is the oldest trout hatchery in the southern hemisphere. Now a museum, it is still used for breeding Tasmanian trout.

7 Subsequent attempts at establishing Atlantic salmon in Tasmania and elsewhere in the Antipodes also failed.

8 Paul Schullery, 'Imperialist Trout', first published in *American Angler* magazine (2005): www.midcurrent.com/articles/history/schullery_imperialist_trout.aspx (accessed 6 May 2011).

9 John Mitchinson, 'QI Book of the Dead: Exclusive Extracts from the Brains Behind the TV Show', *The Daily Telegraph* (24 November 2009).

10 Christopher Lever, *The Naturalized Animals of the British Isles* (London, 1977), p. 30.

11 Christopher Lever, *They Dined on Eland: The Story of the Acclimatisation Societies* (London, 1992), pp. 74–7.

12 Ibid., pp. 102–3.

13 Nicols, *The Acclimatisation of the Salmonidae at the Antipodes*, p. 2.

14 Ibid., p. 2.

15 Ibid., p. 4.

16 Ibid., p. 91.

17 R. C. Lamb, *Beasts, Birds and Fishes: The First Hundred Years of the North Canterbury Acclimatisation Society* (Christchurch, New Zealand, 1964), p. 33.

18 Robert M. Poole, 'Fish Story', *Smithsonian* magazine (August 2007): www.smithsonianmag.com/science-nature/trout_main.html (accessed 21 September 2011).

19 'Midsummer Beaverkill Fishing', *New York Times* (15 July 1894).

20 Schullery, 'Imperialist Trout'.

21 Wang Zhaoming and Yang Yuhui, 'Cold Water Fish Culture in China', from *Cold Water Fisheries in the Trans-Himalayan Countries*, published in 2002 by the Food and Agriculture Organization of the United Nations: www.fao.org/docrep/005/Y3994E/y3994e0b.htm (accessed 19 May 2011).

22 Chen Xiaorong, 'The Call of Yanxi Rainbow Trout', *China Daily* (26 June 2008).

23 Silvio Calabi, *Trout and Salmon of the World* (Secaucus, NJ, 1990), p. 109.

24 S. J. Lowe, M. Browne and S. Boudjelas, *100 of the World's Worst Invasive Alien Species*, published in Auckland, New Zealand, 2000, by the IUCN/SSC Invasive Species Specialist Group.

25 Richard Yallop, 'Values clash over invasive trout is becoming elevated to national policy level in Australia' *The Australian* (2 January 2004).

26 Peter Rolfe, 'Trout Declared an "Alien Species"', *Sunday Herald Sun* (30 December 2007).

27 Katherine Ross, *Freshwater Fish in the Falklands: Conservation of Native Zebra Trout*, report to the Falkland Islands Government and Falklands Conservation (2009).

28 Roland A. Knapp, 'The Mountain Yellow-Legged Frog Site': www.mylfrog.info/index.html (accessed 19 May 2011).

29 V. T. Vredenburg, et al., 'Concordant Molecular and Phenotypic Data Delineate New Taxonomy and Conservation Priorities for the Endangered Mountain Yellow-legged Frog', *Journal of Zoology*, CCLXXI/4 (April 2007), pp. 361–74.

30 Anders Halverson, *An Entirely Synthetic Fish: How Rainbow Trout Beguiled America and Overran the World* (New Haven, CT, 2010), p. 88.

31 Ibid., p. 88.
32 Ibid., p. 89.
33 Ibid., p. 91.
34 Claude M. Kreider, 'It's Raining Baby Trout', *Popular Mechanics Magazine* (July 1954), p. 120.
35 Halverson, *An Entirely Synthetic Fish*, p. 91.
36 R. A. Knapp, D. M. Boiano, and V. T. Vredenburg, 'Removal of Nonnative Fish Results in Population Expansion of a Declining Amphibian', *Biological Conservation*, CXXXV/1 (February 2007), pp. 11–20.
37 R. A. Knapp, 'Effects of Nonnative Fish and Habitat Characteristics on Lentic Herpetofauna in Yosemite National Park, USA', *Biological Conservation*, CXXI/2 (2005), pp. 265–79.
38 Colden V. Baxter, et al., 'Fish Invasion Restructures Stream and Forest Food Webs by Interrupting Reciprocal Prey Subsidies', *Ecology*, LXXXV/10 (October 2004), pp. 2656–63.
39 David Quammen, 'The Weeds Shall Inherit the Earth', *The Independent* (22 November 1998).
40 Clint C. Muhlfeld, et al., 'Hybridization Rapidly Reduces Fitness of a Native Trout in the Wild', *Biology Letters*, V/3 (June 2009), pp. 328–31.
41 Personal communication.
42 Contrary to popular belief, a species can be considered distinct even if it is capable of breeding with other, related species. Trout are a case in point.
43 Personal communication.
44 Poole, 'Fish Story'.
45 Schullery, 'Imperialist Trout'.

4 FILLETED TROUT

1 Michelle Berriedale-Johnson, *The British Museum Cookbook* (London, 1995), p. 65.
2 Juliana Berners, *A Treatyse of Fysshynge Wyth an Angle* (London, 1496). Part of the *Boke of Saint Albans*, a sporting volume complied

and published by Wynkyn de Worde, the *Treatyse* is celebrated as the earliest text on angling in printed English.

3 Izaak Walton and Charles Cotton, *The Compleat Angler* [1676] (London 1844), p. 66.

4 Thomas Barker, *The Art of Angling* [1653] (Leeds, 1817), pp. 13–14.

5 The fifth and final edition of *Compleat Angler* in 1676 included a second part on fly-fishing written by Walton's friend and fishing partner Charles Cotton.

6 Walton and Cotton, *The Compleat Angler*, pp. 346–7.

7 Alan Davidson, *The Oxford Companion to Food* (Oxford, 1999), p. 40.

8 Patricia Ann Hayes, *The Trout Cook: 100 Ways with Trout* (Marlborough, 1998).

9 Juliet Clough, 'Oslo: A City Worth Screaming About', *The Daily Telegraph* (18 January 1997).

10 While *rakørret* (trout) is the most commonly eaten type of '*rakfisk*', fish such as char and whitefish are prepared this way as well.

11 Andreas Viestad, 'Making Gravlax: No Longer an Underground Art', *The Washington Post* (23 September 2009).

12 Harry E. Wedeck, 'Trout', in *Dictionary of Aphrodisiacs* [1962] (London, 1994), p. 237.

13 L. Patrick Coyle, *The World Encyclopedia of Food* (New York, 1982), p. 690.

14 Norman Smith, 'The Roman Dams of Subiaco', *Technology and Culture*, XI/1 (1970), pp. 58–68.

15 Rodolfo Lanciani, *Ancient Rome in the Light of Recent Discoveries* (Boston, MA, 1888), p. 274.

16 Augustus John Cuthbert Hare, *Days Near Rome*, vol. I (London, 1875), p. 294.

17 R. J. Zeepvat, *Medieval Fish, Fisheries and Fishponds in England*, ed. Michael Aston (Oxford, 1988), p. 23.

18 Ibid.

19 John Taverner, *Certaine Experiments Concerning Fish and Fruite* [1600] (London, 1928), pp. 6–15.

20 Some question the existence of the fifteenth-century manuscript that attributes the discovery of artificial fish propagation to Dom

Pinchon. The manuscript was cited in the nineteenth century by the Baron de Montgaudry, but, writes Darin Kinsey, 'he never produced the document, and his claim came to be viewed by many outside of France as spurious', Darin Kinsey, '*Seeding the Water as the Earth*: The Epicenter and Peripheries of a Western Aquacultural Revolution', *Environmental History*, XI/3 (2006), pp. 527–66.

21 Francis Francis, *Fish-culture: A Practical Guide to the Modern System of Breeding and Rearing Fish* (London, 1865), p. 4.

22 Herbert Spencer Davis, *Culture and Diseases of Game Fishes* (Berkeley, CA, 1965), pp. 5–6.

23 Ibid., p. 6.

24 Darin Kinsey, '*Seeding the Water as the Earth*, pp. 527–66.

25 Ibid.

26 Davis, *Culture and Diseases of Game Fishes*, p. 6.

27 Ibid., p. 6.

28 Kinsey, *Seeding the Water as the Earth*, pp. 527–66.

29 Ibid.

30 Ibid.

31 Ibid.

32 Davis, *Culture and Diseases of Game Fishes*, p. 6.

33 Ibid., p. 7.

34 Kinsey, *Seeding the Water as the Earth*, pp. 527–66.

35 Ibid.

36 Ibid.

37 Ibid.

38 Ibid.

39 Food and Agriculture Organization (FAO) of the United Nations, 'Oncorhyncus mykiss': www.fao.org/fishery/culturedspecies/Oncorhynchus_mykiss/en (accessed 19 May 2011).

40 'United States Trout Farmers Association': www.ustfa.org/consumers/about.html (accessed 19 May 2011).

41 Anders Halverson, *An Entirely Synthetic Fish: How Rainbow Trout Beguiled America and Overran the World* (New Haven, CT, 2010), p. 59.

42 Ibid., p. 34.

43 Ibid., p. 39.

44 Theodore Gordon, *Theodore Gordon on Trout*, ed. Paul Schullery (Mechanicsburg, PA, 2007), p. 62.

45 FAO, 'Oncorhyncus mykiss'.

46 Ibid.

47 Halverson, *An Entirely Synthetic Fish*, p. 73.

48 Ibid., p. 78.

49 David J. Solomon, 'The Potential for Restocking Using All-female Triploid Brown Trout to Avoid Genetic Impact upon Native Stocks', *Trout News*, 23 (January 2003), pp. 28–31.

50 James Owen, 'Genetically Altered Trout Approved for Release in the UK', *National Geographic News* (April 2008): http://news .nationalgeographic.com/news/2008/04/080430-fish-release .html (accessed 20 May 2011).

51 Sara Nelson, 'Meet Arnie, the Terminator Trout with the Physique of a Body-builder', *Daily Mail* (12 March 2010).

52 James Owen, 'Bulging Mutant Trout Created: More Muscle, More Meat', *National Geographic News* (March 2010): http:// news.nationalgeographic.com/news/2010/03/100329-six-pack-mutant-trout-genetically-engineered-modified-gm (accessed 21 September 2011).

53 Personal communication.

54 At the time of writing (early 2011), the US Food and Drug Administration was considering whether to approve the first transgenic animal for human consumption, a fish trademarked as the AquAdvantage salmon.

55 Maxine Frith, 'Eat Fish "or Evolution May Go into Reverse"', *Press Association* (23 May 2000).

56 Ibid.

57 Coyle, *The World Encyclopedia of Food*, p. 689.

58 Hugh Fearnley-Whittingstall, *The River Cottage Cookbook* (London, 2003), p. 322.

1 Ted Hughes, foreword to David Profumo, *In Praise of Trout* (London, 1989), p. ix.

2 Fred Buller and Hugh Falkus, *Falkus and Buller's Freshwater Fishing* (London, 1988), p. 254.

3 Ernest Schwiebert, in a speech given in 2005 at the opening of the American Museum of Fly Fishing at its new home in Manchester, Vermont.

4 Hughes, foreword to *In Praise of Trout*, p. ix.

5 Andrew Herd, *The Fly* (Ellesmere, UK, 2003), p. 25.

6 Ibid., p. 28.

7 Ibid., p. 29.

8 Ibid., p. 30.

9 Juliana Berners, *A Treatyse of Fysshynge Wyth an Angle*, from *The Boke of St Albans* [1496] (London, 1561).

10 Herd, *The Fly*, pp. 58–9.

11 Izaak Walton and Charles Cotton, *The Compleat Angler* [1676] (London 1844), pp. 317–41.

12 Ibid., pp. 318–21.

13 Ibid., p. 329.

14 Sir Humphry Davy, *Salmonia; or, Days of Fly Fishing* [1828] (London, 1851), p. 22.

15 Jungle cock and golden pheasant are a common feature of many traditional wet fly patterns still fished by British trout anglers.

16 A. Courtney Williams, 'Tup's Indispensable', in *A Dictionary of Trout Flies* (London, 1949), pp. 317–20. Williams notes that this unusual source of wool for making trout flies had been used before. In *The Driffield Angler* (Derby, 1806), Alexander Mackintosh recommends for the body of the Green Drake, 'a little fine wool from the ram's testicles, which is of a beautiful dusty yellow'.

17 Buller and Falkus, *Freshwater Fishing*, pp. 259–60.

18 Herd, *The Fly*, p. 296.

19 F. M. Halford, *Dry-Fly Fishing: Theory and Practice* (London, 1889), p. 42.

20 Herd, *The Fly*, pp. 303–4.

21 Ibid. pp. 79–81.

22 Walton and Cotton fished together on the river Dove, which flowed through Cotton's estate in Derbyshire.

23 Dapping can be done with artificial flies as well as natural insects. Traditional Scottish dapping flies are so large and bushy some anglers refer to them as 'shaving brushes'.

24 Walton and Cotton, *The Compleat Angler*, p. 114.

25 Anna Harris, *Trout Fishing in 2006: A Demographic Description and Economic Analysis*, US Fish and Wildlife Service (Arlington, VA, 2010), p. 3.

26 The author of the report, Anna Harris, says the decline in the number of US trout anglers between 1996 and 2006 may be related to the aging of the baby boom generation. Harris, *Trout Fishing in 2006*, p. 12.

27 Ibid., p. 4.

28 Ibid.

29 Ibid.

30 Nader Asgary and Alf H. Walle, 'The Cultural Impact of Globalisation: Economic Activity and Social Change', *Cross Cultural Management*, IX/3 (2002), p. 71.

31 Norman Maclean, *A River Runs Through It* [1976] (London, 1993), p. 1.

32 H. Gosnell, J. H. Haggerty, and W. R. Travis, 'Ranchland Ownership Change in the Greater Yellowstone Ecosystem, 1990–2001: Implications for Conservation', *Society and Natural Resources*, XIX/8 (2006), pp. 743–58.

33 David Stauth, 'Wealthy "Amenity" Ranchers Taking over the West', Oregon State University media release (25 October 2006).

34 Harris, *Trout Fishing in 2006*.

35 Matt Spetalnick, 'Something Fishy About Obama's Montana Visit', *Reuters* (14 August 2009): http://blogs.reuters.com/frontrow/2009/08/14/something-fishy-about-obamas-montana-visit (accessed 19 May 2011).

36 Tom Chandler, 'The Trout Underground' (fly fishing blog;

20 May 2007): http://troutunderground.com/2007/05/20/
an-underground-review-trout-bum-diaries-ii-kiwi-camo (accessed
19 May 2011).

37 Mark Robinson, *Channel 4/The Sunday Times 100 Greatest TV Ads*
(London, 2000).

38 Gary Dexter, 'Title Deed: How the Book got its Name', *The Daily
Telegraph* (27 September 2009).

39 Justine Gaunt, 'Fishing for an Answer to Youth Crime', *Yorkshire
Post* (30 August 2007).

40 Thomas Pero, 'Poet, Pike and a Pitiful Grouse', *The Guardian*
(8 January 1999).

41 Ekrem Sezik, et al., 'Traditional Medicine in Turkey VII: Folk
Medicine in East Anatolia; Erzurum, Erzíncan, Ağri, Kars, Iğdir
Provinces', *Economic Botany*, LI/3 (July 1997), pp. 195–211.

42 Anders Halverson, *An Entirely Synthetic Fish: How Rainbow Trout
Beguiled America and Overran the World* (New Haven, CT, 2010),
pp. 68–71.

43 Oliver Wendell Holmes, *The Works of Oliver Wendell Holmes*
(Boston, MA, 1892), p. 170.

44 From a speech given by Theodore Roosevelt in Chicago, Illinois,
on 10 April 1899. See, for example: http://www.bartleby.com/
58/1.html (accessed 21 September 2011).

45 Halverson, *An Entirely Synthetic Fish*, p. 69.

46 'Field Sports', *New York Times* (12 January 1874).

47 Charles Hallock, *The Fishing Tourist* (New York, 1873) pp. 25–6.

48 Ibid.

49 Gordon Williams, *A Dictionary of Sexual Language and Imagery
in Shakespearean and Stuart Literature* (London, 1994), p. 1238.

50 George Melly, *Hooked!: Fishing Memories* (London, 2001).

51 Richard Brautigan, *Trout Fishing in America* [1967] (London, 1972),
pp. 57–8.

52 Ernest Hemingway, 'Big Two-Hearted River', *The Nick Adams
Stories* (New York, 1980), p. 112.

53 Ernest Hemingway, *Now I Lay Me, Men Without Women* [1928]
(London, 1972), p. 101.

54 Hemingway, *Big Two-Hearted River*, p. 105.

55 Gregory S. Sojka, *Ernest Hemingway: The Angler as Artist* (New York, 1985), p. 87.

56 Ernest Hemingway, *For Whom the Bell Tolls* [1940] (London, 2004), pp. 455–6.

57 Ernest Hemingway, *The Sun Also Rises* [1928] (New York, 1954), p. 119.

58 Ibid., p. 128.

59 Sojka, *Ernest Hemingway*, p. 71.

60 Brad Hayden, 'Echoes of Walden in *Trout Fishing in America*', *Thoreau Quarterly Journal* (July 1976), pp. 21–6.

61 Brautigan, *Trout Fishing in America*, p. 3.

62 Ibid., p. 41.

63 Ibid., pp. 139–40.

64 Brautigan was part of the community of artists and writers in San Francisco's Haight-Ashbury district which in 1967 hosted the 'Summer of Love' gathering.

65 William Faulkner, *The Sound and the Fury* (New York, 1929), p. 143.

66 Cormac McCarthy, *The Road* [2006] (London, 2009), p. 30.

67 Ibid., p. 42.

68 Ibid., pp. 306–7.

6 WILD TROUT

1 Ted Hughes, foreword to David Profumo, *In Praise of Trout* (London, 1989), p. x.

2 Christopher Camuto, 'Blue Ridge Complex', *The Gift of Trout*, ed. Ted Leeson (New York, 1996), pp. 21–31.

3 Ted Leeson, *The Gift of Trout*, p. viii.

4 Robert M. Poole, 'Hidden Depths', *Smithsonian* (May 2008).

5 John K. Townsend, *Narrative of a Journey across the Rocky Mountains to the Columbia River* (Boston, MA, 1839), pp. 78–9.

6 Patrick Trotter, *Cutthroat: Native Trout of the West* (Berkeley, CA, 2008), p. 7.

7 John H. Monnett, 'Mystery of the Bighorns: Did a Fishing Trip
   Seal Custer's Fate?', *The American Fly Fisher* (Fall 1993).

8 John G. Bourke, *On the Border with Crook* (New York, 1891), pp. 328–9.

9 Trotter, *Cutthroat: Native Trout of the West*, pp. 256–7.

10 Bourke, *On the Border with Crook*, pp. 340–41.

11 Ibid., p. 330.

12 Izaak Walton and Charles Cotton, *The Compleat Angler* [1676]
   (London, 1844), p. 14.

13 Ibid., p. 201.

14 Leslie Dunkling and Gordon Wright, *The Dictionary of Pub Names*
   (Ware, UK, 2006).

15 Charles Kingsley, *Westward Ho!* (Boston, MA, 1855), p. 111.

16 Richard Jefferies, *Nature Near London* [1883] (London, 2010),
   pp. 68–79.

17 Garry Fry, Ivar Muniz and Arnie Semb, 'Nice Video, Shame
   About the Fish', *New Scientist* (27 March 1986).

18 James Owen, '"Fossil Trout" Faces Extinction in Balkans, Experts
   Warn', *National Geographic News* (15 September 2003):
   http://news.nationalgeographic.com/news/2003/09/0915_0309
   15_ohridtrout.html (accessed 20 May 2011).

19 Anonymous, *Balkans: Regional Reporting and Sustainable Training*,
   BCR, 570 (9 August 2005).

20 Aleksandar Nacev, World Bank. Personal communication.

21 *Rivers on the Edge*, WWF-UK campaign (May 2009). For the accompanying report see:
   http://assets.wwf.org.uk/downloads/rivers_on_the_edge.pdf.

22 James Owen, 'Sea Trout Loss Linked to Salmon Farm Parasite',
   National Geographic News (22 October 2002):
   http://news.nationalgeographic.com/news/2002/10/
   1022_021022_seatroutfish.html (accessed 19 May 2011).

23 Ibid.

24 A summary of studies linking sea lice infestation of sea trout to
   salmon farming is contained in the briefing paper by the Salmon
   and Trout Association, 'Impacts of Salmon Aquaculture on Native
   Salmonids Fisheries and the Aquatic Environment' (2010):

www.salmon-trout.org/pdf/STA_the_Impact_of_Salmon_
Aquaculture_Briefting_Paper.pdf (accessed 19 May 2011).

25 Salmon and Trout Association, 'Aquaculture Policy Statement'
(2010): www.salmon-
trout.org/pdf/Aquaculture_Policy_Statement_Final.pdf
(accessed 19 May 2011).

26 Kim Barto, 'Too Warm for Trout?', *Compass* (a publication of the
US Forest Service) (10 February 2008), pp. 20–21.

27 Steven Kinsella, 'The Impacts of Global Warming on Trout in the
Interior West', report for the Natural Resources Defense Council
(July 2008), see:
http://www.nrdc.org/globalwarming/trout/ftrout.pdf.

28 Robert Behnke speaking to Robert M. Poole, 'Fish Story',
Smithsonian (August 2007).

29 Brian Clarke, 'The Myopia that Poses a Threat to Our Passion',
The Times (1 December 2008).

30 Humphry Davy, *Salmonia; or, Days of Fly Fishing* [1828] (London,
1851), pp. 7–8.

31 Ibid., p. 282.

32 John Ruskin, *The Crown of Wild Olive: Three Lectures on Work,
Traffic, and War* (New York, 1866), pp. iii–iv.

33 James Owen, 'All Eyes on the Fry', *The Times* (16 November 2002).

34 James Owen, 'Urban Fishing Catches On in Rebounding Rivers',
National Geographic News (17 May 2010): http://news.national-
geographic.com/news/2010/05/100517-fish-urban-river-
restoration-water (accessed 19 May 2011).

35 Ibid.

Select Bibliography

Alexandersson, Olof, *Living Water: Viktor Schauberger and the Secrets of Natural Energy* (Bath, 1990)

Batchelor, John, *The Ainu and their Folk-lore* (London, 1901)

Behnke, Robert J., *About Trout* (Guilford, CT, 2007)

Bord, Janet, and Colin Bord, *Sacred Water: Holy Wells and Water Lore in Britain and Ireland* (London, 1985)

Bourke, John G., *On the Border with Crook* (New York, 1891)

Brautigan, Richard, *Trout Fishing in America* (San Francisco, CA, 1967)

Calabi, Silvio, *Trout and Salmon of the World* (Secaucus, NJ, 1990)

Coates, Peter, *Salmon* (London, 2006)

Coats, Callum, *Living Energies: Viktor Schauberger's Brilliant Work with Natural Energy Explained* (Dublin, 2001)

Davy, Humphry, *Salmonia; or, Days of Fly Fishing* (London, 1828)

Frost, W. E., and M. E. Brown, *The Trout* (London, 1967)

Gierach, John, *Trout Bum* (Boulder, CO, 1986)

Halford, F. M., *Dry-Fly Fishing: Theory and Practice* (London, 1889)

Halverson, Anders, *An Entirely Synthetic Fish: How Rainbow Trout Beguiled America and Overran the World* (New Haven, CT, 2010)

Hemingway, Ernest, *The Nick Adams Stories* (New York, 1972)

Herd, Andrew, *The Fly* (Ellesmere, 2003)

Jefferies, Richard, *Nature Near London* (London, 1883)

Kingsley, Charles, *The Water-Babies: A Fairy Tale for a Land-baby* (London, 1863)

Kinsey, Darin, '"Seeding the water as Earth": The Epicentre and Peripheries of a Western Agricultural Revolution', *Environmental*

History, XI/3 (2006), pp. 527–66

Leeson, Ted, ed., *The Gift of Trout* (New York, 1996)

Lever, Christopher, *They Dined on Eland: The Story of the Acclimatisation Societies* (London, 1992)

McCarthy, Cormac, *The Road* (New York, 2006)

McGuane, Thomas, *The Longest Silence* (New York, 1999)

Nicols, Arthur, *The Acclimatisation of the Salmonidae at the Antipodes* (London, 1882)

Profumo, David, *In Praise of Trout* (London, 1989)

Taverner, John, *Certaine Experiments Concerning Fish and Fruite* (London, 1600)

Trotter, Patrick, *Cutthroat: Native Trout of the West* (Berkeley, CA, 2008)

Walker, Jean, *Origins of the Tasmanian Trout* (Hobart, Australia, 1998)

Walton, Izaak, and Charles Cotton, *The Compleat Angler* (London, 1676)

Associations and Websites

A Fly Fishing History
Andrew Herd's fascinating site on the history of fly-fishing going back to ancient times is mine of information for students of the sport.
www.flyfishinghistory.com

Salmon and Trout Association
Lobbies on behalf of anglers and fisheries for the sustainable management and protection of salmon and trout in the UK. Useful resource for information on such issues as salmon farming and water extraction.
www.salmon-trout.org

The Sea Trout Group
A Scottish campaign group fighting to save sea trout populations from the impacts of salmon farming.
www.seatroutgroup.org.uk

Trout in the Classroom
This environmental education programme run in schools in America brings conservation into the classroom by enabling kids to raise trout from eggs to fingerlings.
www.troutintheclassroom.org

Trout Unlimited
Trout Unlimited has as its mission 'conserving, protecting and restoring North America's coldwater fisheries and their watersheds'. It has

more than 135,000 volunteers organized into about 400 chapters, and a very informative website.
www.tu.org

Wild Trout Trust
Dedicated to the conservation and protection of wild trout in Britain and Ireland, it provides a valuable service in the form of surveys and expert advice for those seeking to improve and restore wild trout habitat.
www.wildtrout.org

The Wandle Trust
An environmental charity working to return London's much-abused but recovering river Wandle to its former glories as a trout stream. Volunteers regularly meet for 'community cleanups' up and down the river.
www.wandletrust.org

Acknowledgements

Since the foundations for this book were laid many years before I had the idea of writing it, I should first acknowledge my late father, a wonderful fisherman and keen amateur naturalist who took me in search of trout and led me into their watery world.

I must also thank the following for their help in tracking down information and for either the sourcing of images or their kind permission in allowing me to reproduce them in the book: Melinda Byrd, Callum Coats, Enrico Dugina, Robert Falk, Sascha Hallett, Paul Hartlieb, Julie Kipfer, Jeffrey Lentz, Daniel Luther, Heinz Machacek, Gillies Mackenzie, David Mårding, Joe McGowan, Audun Øygard, Theo Pike, Claire Sargent, Jörg Schauberger, Henning Stilke, Erik Weber, Mark Wilson, Dan Vermillion and Goro Yoshizaki. Lastly, a big thanks to Blanche Craig, Susannah Jayes, Michael Leaman and Jonathan Burt for bringing the book to fruition.

Photo Acknowledgements

The author and the publishers wish to extend their thanks to the below sources of illustrative material and/or permission to reproduce it. (Some sources uncredited in the captions for reasons of brevity are also given below.)

Photo courtesy of the Aquaria Vattenmuseum, Stockholm: pp. 23–5; Art Resource, New York: p. 81 (Erich Lessing); Photo courtesy of Blinker Magazine: p. 27 (right); © The Trustees of the British Museum: p. 43; The Cleveland Museum of Art: p. 141 (top); Photo courtesy of Robert Falk: p. 79; Fine Arts Museums of San Francisco: p. 139; Photo courtesy of Trøsvik Gård, Norway: p. 84; Courtesy of Sascha Hallett: p. 100; Oishi Kuranosuke: p. 53; Gilles Mackenzie: p. 150; Image Courtesy of Joe McGowan, www.sweetwatertravel.com: p. 45; Courtesy of the Mid-Continent Railway Historical Society: p. 96; Museum of the City of New York: p. 142; Museum of Fine Arts, Boston: p. 141 (centre); Museo della Pesca, Caslano, Switzerland: p. 27 (left); James Owen: pp. 15, 17, 19, 22, 30, 44, 77, 89 102, 105, 118–19, 153; Rex Features: p. 6 (Brian Pelkey/Solent News), 68 (beddall); Photo courtesy of Claire Sargent: p. 47; Copyright Schauberger-Archive, Bad Ischl, Austria: pp. 38–9; Official White House photo by Pete Souza: p. 122; Courtesy of the State Library of South Australia: p. 61 (slsa: prg 1373/19/36); Copyright Touchstone Distributing, Inc., DeWitt, Mitchigan: p. 48; Photo courtesy of www.TravelTheUnkown.com: p. 50; US Fish and Wildlife Service: pp. 18 (Timothy Knepp), 21, 95 (Eric Engbretson); University of Rhode Island: p. 103; Photograph copyright of the Warburg Institute,

Index

A River Runs Through It 9, 120–23
acclimatization societies 63–5, 67
acid rain 147
Aelian 107
Africa 58, 63, 69
Ainu people 8, 49–53
Albania 148
angling 7, 9–10, 26, 29–30, 54–5,
    68, 70, 96, 107–25, 139–44,
    149, 151–2, 154
Angling Exploration Group 123
aquaculture 9, 80, 82, 85–106,
    149–50
Aquaria Vattenmuseum,
    Stockholm 22–23, 25
Argentina 58, 67, 69, 71
art 42, 57, 141
artificial propagation 8, 33, 88–92
Atlas mountains 16, 20
Australia 8, 20, 58–66, 70
Austria 34, 139

Baltic Sea 22–3
Barker, Thomas 80–82
Batchelor, John 49–53

Battle of the Little Bighorn 142
Behnke, Robert 13, 30, 152
Berners, Juliana 109
Big Two-Hearted River 131, 136
biomimicry 33–40
biotic homogenization 75–8
Blue Ridge Mountains 138
Boerner, Arno 33
Bourke, John 143
Brautigan, Richard 9, 130–31,
    133–5
British Columbia 15
brook trout (*Salvelinus fontinalis*)
    20–21, 30, 68, 75, 137–40
brown trout (*Salmo trutta*) 11–16,
    19–20, 21, 26, 29–30, 41,
    58–71, 75, 77, 147
Buckland, Frank 61, 63
bull trout 20, 22, 151
Buller, Fred 107, 116

Calabi, Silvio 70
California 17–18, 71–3, 95
California Department of Fish
    and Game 72

Camuto, Christopher 138
Canada 15, 20, 56, 99, 126
carp 20, 69, 70, 87–8, 98
Caspian trout 26
Casting for Recovery 126
catch-and-release (angling) 55,
    152
*Certaine Experiments Concerning
    Fish and Fruite* 87
chalkstreams 26, 49, 112, 115–16,
    149, 152
char 20, 64, 69, 75
cherry trout 18–19
China 53, 69
Clark, William 17
Cogan, Thomas 80, 128
Compleat Angler, The 21, 110, 144
Coste, Victor 91–2
Cotton, Charles 82, 110–112, 118
Crook, George 142–3
cutthroat trout (*Oncorhynchus
    clarkii*) 17–18, 21, 29, 75–7
    Alvord cutthroat 77
    Rio Grande cutthroat 18
    westslope cutthroat 75–7

dapping (fishing method) 118
Darwin, Charles 9, 11, 14–15
Davy, Humphry 14, 112, 152
de Worde, Wynkyn 108
diseases (of trout) 55, 99–100,
    119
Devon 146

Eosalmo driftwoodensis 15–16

eutrophication 147–8
evolution 9, 11–16

Falkland Islands 20, 66, 71
Falkus, Hugh 107, 116
Faulkner, William 135
Fibreno trout 19
fish farming *see* aquaculture
fishing tackle 118–19
Fearnley-Whittingstall, Hugh 105
Ferguson, Andrew 14
ferox trout 14
Flyfishers' Club, London 125–6
fly-fishing 7, 9, 26, 107–25, 140,
    152, 154
folklore and religion 8, 42–55
food (trout as) 41, 52, 65, 80–85,
    88–91, 93, 98, 102–6, 142–3
fossil record 15–16
France 9, 63, 85, 88–93
Francis, Francis 61
frog 26–7, 70–71, 73–4
furry or fur-bearing trout 56

Géhin, Antoine 90–91
genetically modified trout 9, 31,
    101–3
Germany 26, 33, 37, 88, 93
Gierach, John 7, 33
Gila trout 32, 77
gillaroo trout 14–15
global warming 151
golden trout 18–19, 77
Gordon, Theodore 96
grayling 19, 64, 110

hairy trout 55–57
Halford, Frederic 115–18
Halverson, Anders 72, 93, 101, 126
Hampshire 115, 117
Hansen, Michael 78
Hartley, J. R. 125, 129
Haven of Health, The 80, 128
Hayden, Brad 133–4
Hemingway, Ernest 9, 131–2, 135
Herd, Andrew 108
Hitler, Adolf 37
Holmes, Charles 11–12
holy wells and springs 8, 42–49
Homer, Winslow 140–41
Hughes, Ted 107, 126, 138
Huningue, France 91–92

Iceland 16, 55
India 20, 58, 66
Ireland 9, 13–14, 46–9, 118, 126
Isle of Skye 45
Italy 19, 86, 131

Jacobi, Stephan Ludwig 88–90
Japan 8, 18, 49–53, 74–5
Jefferies, Richard 146–7
Jeremy Fisher (*The Tale of Mr Jeremy Fisher*) 26–8

Kingsley, Charles 27–8, 146
Kinsey, Darin 89–92
Korea 18
Knapp, Roland 71, 74

lakes
    Chiemsee 26
    Chitose 52
    Iceberg 57
    Kanas 53
    Maggiore 26
    Ohrid 148
    Posta Fibreno 19
    lake trout 20
Leeson, Ted 139
lenok 20
Lewis, Meriwether 17
Linnaeus, Carl 11
literature 48, 107, 121, 129–37, 139
Loch Maree, Scotland 149
London 146, 151
Lough Melvin, Ireland 9, 13–14

Macedonia 148
Maclean, Norman 121
Maine 68, 140
marble trout 19, 78
Martin, Martin 45–6
mayflies 26, 28, 108, 111–15, 118
McCarthy, Cormac 10, 136–7
McGuane, Thomas 10
Melly, George 129–30
Mexico 18
Michigan 131
Mongolia 20, 53–55,
Montana 121–3
Montana State University 122–3
Morocco 20
music 139–40

Native Americans 142–3
Nature Near London 146–7
Nelson, Horatio 152
Nero (Roman emperor) 86
Nevada 71
New Mexico 17–18
New York state 68, 140
New Zealand 20, 60, 65–7,
    69–70, 79, 126
Nicols, Arthur 60, 65–6
Norway 83–4, 147

Obama, Barack 122–3
Ohrid trout 148
On the Origin of Species 11
Oncorhynchus clarkii
    see cutthroat trout
Oncorhynchus mykiss see rainbow
    trout

Peterchurch, Herefordshire 44
Pinchon, Dom 88
Pitt, Brad 121–2
pollution 10, 53, 147–52, 154
Poole, Robert 68, 79, 140–41
Potter, Beatrix 26, 28
Profumo, David 45, 49, 109
pub names and signs 144

Quammen, David 75

rainbow trout (*Oncorhynchus
    mykiss*) 16–18, 21, 30–32,
    68–70, 74–7, 93–106
rakørret (fermented trout) 83–4

Ramsbottom, Robert 59
redband trout 18, 77
Redford, Robert 121
Reese, Al 72
Remy, Joseph 90–91
rivers
    Aniene 86
    Arkansas 56
    Avon (Wiltshire) 49
    Blackfoot 112
    Derwent (Tasmania) 62, 66
    Dore 44
    Dove 27, 118
    East Gallatin 123
    Ewe 149
    Green 142
    Itchen 61, 117
    Kennet 49
    Moselle 85
    Neversink 117
    Test 115
    Thames 62
    Tongue 143
    Usk 129
    Üür 53
    Waimakariri 67
    Wandle 152–4
Road, The 10, 136–7
Rocky Mountains 17, 56, 68, 75,
    151
Romans 85–7,
Roosevelt, Theodore 127–8
Ruskin, John 152–3
Russia 17–18, 94

sabre-tooth salmon 16
Saint Peris 42–3
Salmo trutta see brown trout
salmon 11, 16, 19, 21–2, 24, 32, 52,
    58–67, 93, 127, 149–50
Salmon & Trout Association 150
Salmon Ponds, Tasmania 62–4,
    67
Schauberger, Viktor 9, 34–40
Schubert, Franz 139–40
Schullery, Paul 69, 79
Schwiebert, Ernest 107
Scotland 45–6, 65, 149–50
sea lice 149–50
sea trout 20–23, 25–6, 146,
    149–50
Sierra Nevada mountains 18, 71–3
Shakenoak villa, Oxfordshire
    86–7
Shakespeare, William 129
Skues, G.E.M. 116–18
slob trout 21
Slovenia 19
softmouth trout 19
Sojka, Gregory 133
sonaghan trout 14–15
Song of Wandering Aengus, The 48
Spain 41, 133
Spencer Davis, Herbert 88–9
stocking (of trout) 72–8, 90,
    95–6, 101, 128
Sun Also Rises, The (Hemingway)
    133
Sweden 22, 24
Switzerland 26

taimen 20, 53–5
Tasmania 58–63, 65–6, 70
Taverner, John 87
Tierra del Fuego 67
Thoreau, Henry 133
Tobernalt Holy Well, Ireland 45–7
transgenic trout 9, 31, 102–3
transportation (of trout) 8, 58–63,
    72, 87, 95
*Treatyse of Fysshynge Wyth an
    Angle* 80, 109–10
triploid trout 101–2
Trotter, Patrick 18
trout
    as invasive species 70–75
    as laboratory animals 31–3
    food and diet 26–8
    hybrids 75–7
    life cycle and growth 24–6
    migration 21–3, 77
    reproduction 23–4
    variety 11–21
    vision and senses 28–30
Trout, The (Frost and Brown) 21,
    28–9
Trout Fishing in America 9, 130–31,
    133–5
trout fishing *see* angling,
    fly-fishing
trout flies 107–18
Trout in the Classroom 154
trout tickling 128–30
Trout Unlimited 151
tuna 32–3
Turkey 126

United States Fish Commission
95

Wales 12, 42–4
Walker, Jean 58–62
Walton, Izaak 8, 10, 21, 26, 80,
    82, 98, 110, 112, 118, 142, 144,
    148
Wandle Trust 154
Water-Babies, The 28–9
water extraction 149
Wendell Holmes, Oliver 126
Wild Trout Trust 10, 152
whirling disease *see* diseases
White Trout of Cong 48
Wulff, Lee 151
Wyoming 123, 142–3

Yeats, W. B. 48
Yellowstone Park 142
Yamada, Takeshi 57
Yoshizaki, Goro 32–3
Youl, James 59–62

zebra trout 20, 71